<preparing web graphics>

by: lynda weinman
design: ali karp & lynda weinman

\<preparing web graphics\>

by Lynda Weinman

New Riders Publishing
201 West 103rd Street
Indianapolis, IN 46290 USA

ISBN: 1-56205-686-7
© 1997 by Lynda Weinman
Printed in the United States of America 1 2 3 4 5 6 7 8 9 0
Library of Congress Cataloging-in-Publication Data
•CIP data available upon request•

Warning and Disclaimer

Trademark Acknowledgments

✎	**Publisher**	Don Fowley
✎	**Associate Publisher**	David Dwyer
✎	**Marketing Manager**	Mary Foote
✎	**Managing Editor**	Carla Hall

credits

Senior Acquisitions Editor
John Kane

Project Editor
Jennifer Eberhardt

Senior Editors
Sarah Kearns & Suzanne Snyder

Software Specialist
Steve Flatt

Acquisitions Coordinator
Stacey Beheler

Administrative Coordinator
Karen Opal

Cover Design, Illustrations, and Hand-Tinted Photos
Bruce Heavin
bruce@stink.com
http://www.stink.com

Book Designer
Ali Karp
Alink Newmedia
alink@earthlink.net
http://home.earthlink.net/~alink/

Cover Production
Aren Howell
Production Manager
Kelly Dobbs
Team Supervisors
Laurie Casey & Joe Millay
Production Team
Dan Caparo, Laure Robinson, Megan Wade

Indexer
Tim Wright

the author

Lynda Weinman writes full-time for a living now, but in the past has been a designer, animator, magazine contributor, computer consultant, instructor, moderator, and lecturer. She lives in California with her illustrator husband, Bruce Heavin, seven-year-old daughter, Jamie, and their deeply revered kats, Stinky and Blue. Lynda has taught Web Design, Interactive Media Design, Motion Graphics, 3D Animation, and Digital Imaging at lots of schools and colleges, including Art Center, UCLA, AFI, and San Francisco State Multimedia Studies Program. Lynda contributes regularly to *Web Techniques*, *Web Studio* (in Japan), *Step-by-Step Graphics*, and *MacUser* magazines. Lynda keeps an up-to-date web site at

http://www.lynda.com

To my treasured daughter, **Jamie**, and husband, **Bruce**, who put up with my obsessive workaholism and love me anyway.

To **Ali**, my book designer and collaborator and friend.

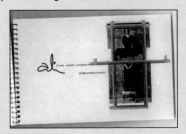

To the terrific **New Riders team**—especially **John Kane** and **Jennifer Eberhardt** who bleed, sweat, cry, and joke with me. Not to forget the incredible David Dwyer, Don Fowley, Mary Foote, Laura Frey, Stacey Beheler, and Steve Flatt.

acknowledgments

To my pal and fellow authoress **Crystal Waters** for knowing how to make me laugh when I'm tired and need a hug.

To the great clip art collections used in this book from **PhotoDisc** (http://www.photodisc.com), **Classic PIO Partners**, (800-370-2746) and the book, **_Mostly Happy Clip Art_** by Jerry Jankowski (ISBN:0-88108-109-4).

To my wonderful, supportive, extremely fuzzy and squeezable husband, **Bruce**, for making art for this and other books, and helping me research more about web graphics than we'd ever want to know.

The design of _Preparing Web Graphics_ pays homage to my 1950's roots, with its idealized visions of the future and gender stereotypes that fortunately didn't come true.

contents at a glance

Introduction 1

1 Getting Started 7

2 Web Environment 25

3 Web File Formats   41

4 Speedy Web Graphics   59

5 Cross-Platform Color   87

6 Transparency 123

7 Background Tiles 139

8 Links, Maps, Frames 149

9 Rules, Bullets, Buttons   169

10 Typography 181

11 Alignment 193

12 Animation 211

web design

Even though web design is in its infancy, an overwhelming number of new skills and tools already exist to learn and master. It's now possible to easily create web pages, but what isn't obvious or easy is learning to make the graphics perform well and look good over multiple platforms, operating systems, and browsers.

It's my belief that visual design plays a huge role in the success of a web site. It's not enough to create a site and post it to the Internet. Your audience will judge your site on its content, appearance, responsiveness, and accessibility.

The web is a publishing medium, and the beauty of it is that anyone can choose to be the audience or the publisher. This, in itself, is revolutionary because there's never been a global, instant publishing medium where anyone could participate. Most new web publishers experience a thrill seeing their work appear on the web for the first time. Once the novelty wears off, however, most people then seek to improve and refine their first efforts.

Introduction

who this book is for

I have been teaching digital design techniques for the past seven years, and have been working professionally in computer graphics and animation using personal computers for the past 16 years. I've written a series of successful professional-level web design books, which were targeted toward existing design professionals who wanted to learn web design techniques. At the same time, many nondesigners have bought and enjoyed my books, too, confirming my belief that the web will introduce a whole new audience to computer graphics.

The truth is that many web publishers are not design professionals and have had no prior design skills with creating visuals before the web came along. This group of people have the most to learn and are the least equipped to do so. I felt it was important to write a book geared specifically to this group—to share the wealth of research, tips, and techniques I've assembled for my other books with this often overlooked audience.

my teaching philosophy

In my years of teaching about computers, I've developed strong principles about how people learn most effectively. Computer graphics can be an overwhelmingly technical subject, but can also be incredibly fun and satisfying once you get beyond the mechanics. I like to get past the technical aspects as quickly as possible, without weighing my students down with every possible fact about each subject. My goal is to cut to the chase and quickly get to what people need to know, as opposed to loading them down with everything there is to know. I like to see my students doing and creating, instead of memorizing facts and technical specifications.

I am not a trained writer; instead I am a trained teacher and designer. My writing style is conversational, and I avoid big words, jargon, and technicalities whenever possible. I try to make no assumptions about the experience level of my reader, and explain principles and concepts as fully as space allows.

how this book works

This book is divided into chapters that build a foundation of knowledge geared to inform you about web graphics issues, techniques, and solutions. Writing about web design is a tricky thing because there are so many overlapping concepts. Sometimes, making the decision about which chapter to put with which subject is difficult! For this reason, I have intentionally structured this book so that readers can approach it in a nonlinear manner. Whenever a subject is mentioned in more than one chapter, it is clearly noted.

Although it might be possible to read or skim this book in a single day, the information inside is far too overwhelming to absorb in a single sitting. It took me many months to write the first *Designing Web Graphics* and many more months to write the second edition. Even with that many months, I could not have possibly understood the task at hand without many more years of experience under my belt as a computer graphics artist and teacher. The task of collecting all this information in one place is enormous and, frankly, never feels finished. The web changes and evolves constantly, but once the ink is dry on this book's pages, it will forever be there.

That's why there are many references to outside information sources in this book. Everything from other URLs, other books, magazines, conferences, newsgroups, mailing lists, and CD-ROMs are offered as support resources whenever a new subject is touched upon. I wrote this book with the full understanding that information will change and evolve, and gave you outside channels to get to that new information. Updates and errata will be posted at my web site as well. Just remember how to spell my name—with a "y"—and you'll be able to e-mail me or check in on my web site at any time. I can't promise to answer everyone, but I do whenever time permits.

 lynda@lynda.com

http://www.lynda.com

3

Which <...ing web graphics> Book Is Right for You?

Now that I've written a slew of books, I get a lot of e-mail from people saying they want to buy one of my books, but aren't sure which one is right for them.

<preparing web graphics> is appropriate for web publishers who are just getting started in the medium. It is a lower-cost alternative to *designing web graphics.2*, and was written to make sure that everyone can afford to access the research and step-by-step lesson plans I've created to make web graphics load quickly, work with cross-platform colors, and understand the constraints and workarounds of the medium. This comprehensive guide includes all the essential information to make your graphics and design work most effectively in an online environment.

<designing web graphics.2> is appropriate for professional designers and web publishers who are planning or already creating web sites. This book is the cornerstone of my series—and covers web design issues from A through Z. *<designing web graphics.2>* is twice as big as *<preparing web graphics>*, and includes more in-depth information about creating graphics and other web-related technologies, such as plug-ins, scripting, and CGI.

tip

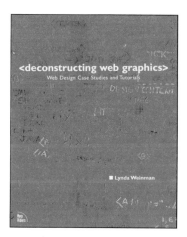

<deconstructing web graphics> approaches learning web design through a different means. Because most of the HTML buffs I know taught themselves through viewing others' source code, I thought it would be great to select from inspirational sites and view their code for readers. Each line of code is explained, and behind-the-scenes profiles are made of programmers, designers, photographers, and illustrators. Everything from Photoshop layers to Shockwave/Lingo files are analyzed and demystified. This book is great for experienced designers looking for inspiration and improvement, and non-hands-on people who want an overview of issues surrounding web design.

<coloring web graphics> is half book, half software. The book is a definitive guide to color on the web. Everything from file compression to dithering to browser-safe colors is thoroughly explained. My co-author, Bruce Heavin, assembled hundreds of suggested color combinations for web sites. The CD-ROM includes swatches that can be loaded into Photoshop, Paint Shop Pro, Painter, Photo-Paint, and FreeHand. The book offers lots of step-by-step tutorials, and the CD-ROM swatches provide endless ideas for successful and cross-platform-compatible color schemes.

summary

Contents at a Glance

Here's a breakdown of the subjects this book covers:

1 Getting Started
Software and hardware advice on
how to get started in web design.

2 Web Environment
Cross-platform computing issues,
as well as equipment and multiple
browser differences.

3 Web File Formats
In-depth coverage of GIFs and JPEGs,
to help you understand when to use
which format.

4 Speedy Web Graphics
Make the smallest possible images
that will download quickly and ensure
high quality.

5 Cross-Platform Color
How, when, and why to use browser-
safe colors. Includes a reference of
color HTML tags and a cross-platform,
hex-compatible chart.

6 Transparency
Create GIF transparency and eliminate
unwanted halos.

7 Background Tiles
Make seamless and seamed tiles
with step-by-step tutorials for
the images and HTML.

8 Links, Maps, Frames
Create images and imagemaps, and
learn to make artwork appear clickable.

9 Rules, Bullets, Buttons
Use HTML code and custom artwork for
rules, bullets, and buttons.

10 Typography
Practical HTML and Photoshop 4.0
examples that address the aesthetics,
techniques, and resources required to
make the best use of web typography.

11 Alignment
Tables? Invisible GIFs? Alignment tags?
You've come to the right chapter.

12 Animation
Shockwave? Animated GIFs? Java-
Script? QuickTime? It's all covered in
this chapter.

learning web design

Web page design is still so new that there are no set rules, standards, or certificates that officially qualify anyone as a web designer. Anyone can do web design, but doing web design well takes some practice and study. If you're feeling insecure about your general design skills or web design skills, you may be wondering whether you can create a successful site on your own. Although web design schools will probably exist someday, for the moment you can get your web design education a few different ways:

- Books, like this one!

- Studying and reverse-engineering successfully designed sites

- Reading other web design books and related magazine articles

- Referencing online web design resources

- Joining web design usenet groups and listservs

- Joining design organizations

- Attending conferences or taking seminars

Getting Started 1

7

using search engines

Search engines allow you to search the web for content, much like the phone book enables you to find phone numbers. Using them offers great ways to find things you need to know about web design (or anything else in the universe, for that matter). If you're looking for advice, tutorials, reviews, or new software or hardware, look to the web first! It's the greatest encyclopedia ever created.

Here are some URLs of my favorite search engines:

✍ http://www.altavista.digital.com

✍ http://www.yahoo.com

✍ http://www.excite.com

✍ http://www.hotbot.com

✍ http://www.webworkstudio.com

Some search engines are database driven, meaning that the entries are submitted and stored in a database. Other search engines use "spiders" that crawl automatically over the web to retrieve pointers to information. Which type of information you're looking for determines which type of search engine to use. It's not always obvious by going to a search engine site which type of method it uses, but if you don't find what you're looking for be sure to check out other search engines that might use different means of gathering information.

As well as knowing which search engines to use, it's very important to know how to use a search engine. Most of the search engines have help-based tutorials that can make all the difference. The goal of a search is to come up with the exact matches you want. Most engines fail to find the correct response or correct number of responses because the search is too broad.

Using ✍ www.altavista.digital.com, for example, I typed Lynda Weinman. The search engine reported 2,487 occurrences of the name Weinman and 20,685 occurrences of the name Lynda. But when I put my name in quotes—"Lynda Weinman"—the search engine knew to report only occurrences of that exact combination of words and yielded the more accurate result of 600.

For a great tutorial on using search engines, try:

✍ http://www.webreference.com/content/search/

✍ http://calafia.com/webmasters

listing with search engines

You can also register your web sites with search engines. This is usually a free but time-consuming process. Here are some URLs to contact:

- http://www.yahoo.com

- http://altavista.digital.com

- http://www.excite.com

- http://www.lycos.com

- http://guide.infoseek.com

- http://www.mckinley.com

- http://www.webcrawler.com

- http://www.opentext.com

- http://www.hotbot.com

- http://www.infomarket.ibm.com

- http://www.nln.com

- http://www.shareware.com

Most likely, you'll need to create a summary of your site, using 25 words or less, to describe "keywords" that others might find you by. For example, if your site is about the new *Star Wars* movie, you might want to include keywords such as: movies, George Lucas, Rebellion, science fiction, Death Star.

If you don't want to do all the work of personally submitting your keywords, try this service, which will submit your site listing to many different search engines:

- http://www.submit-it.com/

equipment and software

All of you, at some point in your web design life, will have to answer some basic questions. What platform should I use? Which software should I get? Which type of HTML editor should I use? How much RAM do I need? What kind of scanner do I need? This chapter walks you through some of these important decisions you'll need to make.

The ideal setup for a web design studio would be to own a Mac, PC, Sun, and SGI; have a full video and sound studio; and own all the imaging, video, sound, and authoring software in the universe. No one will be quite so lucky, but that gives you an idea of how limitless the possibilities are for equipment and software acquisitions!

Given these infinite options, you're going to need some general guidelines. Here they are:

✎   Macs and PCs are going to have the widest range of web-design tools.

✎   Most of your web audience will be on Macs or PCs. So even if you're lucky enough to work on a higher-end Unix platform, you might consider getting one of these lower-end platforms to author web pages. At the very least, working with lower-end platforms will give you a reality checkpoint.

which flavor: mac or pc?

The web is unusual in that no other type of design has ever required such an understanding of cross-platform differences and compatibility issues. Even multimedia developers have always had the option of creating distinct titles for different computer platforms. As evidence, it's very common in the CD-ROM section of store shelves to see two different aisles: one for Mac and one for PCs. Computer stores almost never even have aisles for Unix platforms! But when you're authoring for the web—regardless of which platform you own—you'll be creating material for every platform.

Chances are, you already have a computer. If you don't, and are considering getting one for the purposes of web design, then you have some serious decisions to make. Be forewarned that this is a topic of great passion and controversy. This subject is known to stir up more trouble than a presidential debate!

macs versus pcs

There's a great irony in web design: most professional web designers and art directors are on Macs, but most of the audiences they design for are on PCs. The Mac was the first mainstream operating system to have a GUI (graphical user interface). Because most visual designers go for that sort of thing (myself included), it should be no surprise that we would end up using Macs. Even now that Win95 emulates a lot of that same interface, there are many die-hard Mac users who vow they will never switch. For the time being, the Mac is still the most popular design platform.

I am not suggesting that you should not use or buy a PC. And I am not suggesting that PCs are inferior. I am just stating some facts. It is true that there are many more PCs in circulation than Macs, but it is also true that the Mac is still the most popular platform for visual design folks. Popular doesn't necessarily mean best; it just means the numbers are bigger.

some mac advantages: You'll find that the majority of design-based software comes out on the Mac before the PC. You'll also find that most service bureaus that deal with desktop publishing are biased toward Macs, not PCs. Most likely, you'll find more support among other artists and designers if you are on a Mac.

some pc advantages: Most end users are on PCs. Most browser software comes out first for the PC, and often never fully supports the Mac. The PC has a bigger market share than the Mac, so equipment and peripherals are often less expensive.

There is truly no wrong or right platform. Regardless of which platform you buy, you will be able to design web pages. My suggestion is to try out the software and equipment you want to get before you buy it. Ask around. Find sites that you admire and ask what equipment and software the designers recommend. There's no wrong decision here; just make sure your choice fits your budget, needs, and likes.

It's always important to check your site on platforms other than the one you authored from. If you are lucky enough to own two platforms, this can be done in the luxury of your own office, studio, or home. If not, make sure you locate another system where you can preview your site. As future chapters will describe in detail, what you see on one platform ain't necessarily what you see on others. This is a universal problem and will be the case regardless of which platform you own.

system requirements

Believe it or not, web authoring is not a taxing activity for a computer system. It's not necessary to have the fastest and newest machine, as it is in other disciplines such as desktop publishing, digital video, or 3D rendering. In fact it's possible to get by with much less than the top-of-the-line when it comes to equipment. I recommend that you put your investments in RAM or great imaging software, such as Photoshop, than in the latest and greatest computer model.

Let's break down the key components of a computer system—processor speed, RAM, hard disk, video and sound cards, monitor, CD-ROM drive, modem, and scanner—and evaluate their importance for web authoring.

- **processor speed:** These days, we often hear about fast processor speeds, sometimes even in excess of 500 MHz (megahertz). How important a factor is processing speed in terms of web design? Not very. Processing speed helps with 3D graphics rendering and the speed of rendering television or film-sized movies. It really helps when you're working with a huge, high-resolution image that's being prepped for printing. Processing speed also helps with complex, math-intensive computer operations. But unless you are planning to use your computer for those types of projects in addition to web design, a fast processor is going to buy you very little advantages.

- **ram:** The popular adage for western culture, you can never be too rich or too thin, translates to popular computer culture as: you can never have too much RAM or hard disk space. Having RAM makes it possible to work with multiple software applications. It lets you keep an HTML editor, an imaging program, and a web browser open at the same time. This will save you more time (and isn't your time worth money, too?) than you may imagine. Never skimp on RAM if you can possibly avoid it. A minimum requirement would be 16mb, and maximum would be...? Well, as I said, you can never have too much RAM!

- **hard disks:** You can never have too much hard disk space. Just like a job where the amount of work seems to fill however long the deadline lasts, most projects take up all the hard disk space you have. I highly recommend getting a removable storage system in addition to a permanent hard drive. Zip drives are great; Jaz drives are sublime!

✎ **video cards:** Most computer systems ship with a video card preinstalled. For this reason, many new computer buyers aren't even aware of their video card's features or capabilities. The video card is what dictates how many colors your monitor can display. Most of the web audience has 8-bit color (256 color) or less. Images look much better with millions (24-bit) or thousands (16-bit) of color displays. If you have the chance, go for a card with the highest possible bit depth (24-bit). This enables you to design for everyone—those with the lowest and highest common denominators.

✎ **sound cards:** If you plan to work with sound, you will need a sound card. Again, many contemporary computers ship with these cards built-in. The web today mostly offers 8-bit sound because the files are smaller and faster to download. Regardless—just like with video cards—it's always best to start with the highest quality and downscale for your audience later.

✎ **monitors:** The majority of your audience will be on standard 640×480 monitors. It's much more fun to design on a larger monitor, however, because you can have more room for all the menus, windows, and palettes that most popular imaging programs sport these days. Almost any kind of monitor will do (make sure it will work with the kind of video card you get), but bigger the better for ease of use with design.

✎ **cd-rom drives:** A lot of software these days ships on CDs. They're very handy to have. Installing software from a CD is handy, but if you're using your CD-ROM drive for this purpose only, speed doesn't matter much. If you're going to play games or look at CD-ROM titles, however, you'll want 2X speed at the very least.

✎ **modems:** Picking a modem is often based on price versus performance. I suggest you choose one based on the latter, not the former. The faster the better. If you're uploading files to a web site, you will be grateful for being able to transfer at the fastest possible speed. Getting a modem is not something to skimp on if you're planning on doing this kind of work seriously.

✎ **scanners:** Because you'll be working with low-resolution imagery, dots per inch and image quality are not your primary considerations when choosing a scanner for web design. Speed is the primary concern, so pick a scanner that can scan in color quickly. For the resolution of web images, speed is the only factor that will make any difference in your production flow.

software

Software by nature is fluid. It will always change. That is its purpose! If it stayed the same, we would all complain. This fact doesn't make for a comfortable authoring or learning environment, however. How many other professions or hobbies do you know of where the tools change and evolve constantly? You can bemoan this fact or embrace it. If you plan to participate in the digital arts, changing software is a fact of life.

There are two categories of software: that which you must buy, and that which is free and downloadable from the web. Most likely, you will have to buy software sooner or later, even though at times it seems that everything you could ever want can be found on the web. This section helps you weigh some of the software decisions, makes recommendations, and lists resources.

imaging programs

In order to create graphics for the web, you will need some image-making software. This book concentrates primarily on Photoshop, Painter, Paint Shop Pro, and Photo-Paint techniques.

Among professional designers Photoshop is the most popular imaging software on any platform for almost any purpose—not just web design. Not surprisingly, it also has the most depth and more features than other software packages reviewed in this book. I use Photoshop primarily, and this book is weighed in its favor.

I know, however, that not everyone needs nor can afford professionally priced and feature-based programs such as Photoshop and Painter. For this reason, I've taught myself a couple of other, less-expensive imaging programs: Paint Shop Pro and Photo-Paint. Whenever possible, I'll share imaging techniques in these programs, too.

If you're going to make your living off web design, don't skimp on imaging software. Bite the bullet and buy Photoshop. I have rarely heard of anyone who was sorry they did. Becoming literate in Photoshop is the number-one, most important skill you can possess. There are wonderful books on Photoshop imaging techniques that beautifully augment this book's content.

Here is a list of excellent Photoshop books:

✎ **The Photoshop WOW! Book**
Authors: Linnea Dayton and Jack Davis
Imprint: Peachpit Press
ISBN: 1-56609-178-0
Retail price: $39.95 U.S.

✎ **Adobe Photoshop for Macintosh**
Classroom in a Book
Author: Adobe Press
Imprint: Hayden
ISBN: 1-56830-118-9
Retail Price: $45.00 U.S.

✎ **Imaging Essentials**
Authors: Luanne Seymour Cohen
and Tanya Wendling
Imprint: Adobe Press
ISBN: 1-56830-093-X
Retail Price: $40.00 U.S.

✎ **Designer Photoshop**
Author: Rob Day
Imprint: Random House
ISBN: 679-75326-5
Retail Price: $30.00 U.S.

✎ **Adobe Photoshop:**
A Visual Guide for the Mac
Authors: David Biedney and Bert Monroy
Imprint: Addison Wesley
ISBN: 0-201-48993-7
Retail Price: $34.95 U.S.

shareware and freeware

The web is a great distribution medium. I predict that someday we will get all our software and updates via the web, instead of off retail shelves or from mail order catalogs. One of the coolest things about the web is that it allows the small developer a distribution avenue to write niche-market software.

Some of my favorite web authoring tools came from the web. There are all kinds of imaging, animation, HTML, and browser-related software choices available. A favorite source for this type of software is at ✍ http://www.shareware.com. You can search by software name, company, or type of product.

16

learning HTML

This is not a general, all-purpose HTML book, but it does include HTML techniques when they are relevant to visual design. I recommend that you supplement this book with an HTML book if you are serious about learning how to code. These are my favorites:

Teach Yourself Web Publishing with HTML 3.2 in a Week, Third Edition
Author: Laura Lemay
Imprint: Sams.net
ISBN: 1-57521-192-0
Retail Price: $29.99 U.S.
http://slack.lne.com/Web/Books/HTML/index.html

HTML Quick Reference
Author: Robert Mullen
Imprint: Que
ISBN: 0-7897-0867-1
Retail Price: $19.99 U.S.
http://www.mcp.com/que/developer_expert/htmlqr/

HTML for the World Wide Web: Visual QuickStart Guide
Author: Elizabeth Castro
Imprint: Peachpit Press
ISBN: 0-201-88448-8
Retail price: $17.95 U.S.
http://www.peachpit.com/peachpit/titles/catalog/88448.html

what does HTML look like?

If you've never seen HTML, here's a sample from my home page of what it looks like. HTML has a basic structure, and this sample illustrates some of its key aspects. By the way, studying my code or anyone else's is a great way to teach yourself how to write your own. It's a tried and true method that most HTML experts recommend and practice.

The finished web page, viewed from within a browser.

❶ `<HTML>`
❷ `<HEAD>`
❸ `<TITLE>Lynda's Homegurrrlpage</TITLE>`
`</HEAD>`
❹ `<BODY BACKGROUND="/ltspiralpat.gif"`
❺ `BGCOLOR="CCCCCC" TEXT="003366"`
`LINK="330066" VLINK="663399"`
`ALINK="CC33FF">`
❻ `<CENTER>`
❼ `<IMG SRC="newlogo.gif">`
❽ `<P>`
`<CENTER><IMG SRC="man.gif">`
`<P>`
`</HTML>`

❶ **<HTML>, </HTML>**: All HTML pages begin and end with the open and closed HTML tag.

❷ **<HEAD>**: The **<HEAD>** tag contains header information, such as the title of the page.

❸ **<TITLE>**: The title of the page goes inside the **<TITLE>** tag.

❹ **<BODY>, BACKGROUND**: The **<BODY>** tag is where you set up body elements. In this case, the HTML is requesting **BACKGROUND="/ltspiralpat.gif"**. This instructs the browser to take the ltspiralpat.gif image and repeat it until it fills the screen. The amount of repeats are dictated by the size of the tile and the size of the end user's screen. For more information on background tiles, check out Chapter 7, "Background Tiles."

**file name:
ltspiralpat.gif**

⑤ BGCOLOR, TEXT, LINK, VLINK, ALINK: The **<BODY>** tag is also where you set up web page colors. Below you'll see my color choices for the background color, text, links, visited links, and active links (the color of the link as you depress the mouse button to click on it). These colors are specified by their hexadecimal equivalents of RGB values. If this sounds Greek to you, check out Chapter 5, "Cross-Platform Color."

003366	330066	663399	CC33FF	CCCCCC
R: 0	**R:** 51	**R:** 102	**R:** 204	**R:** 204
G: 51	**G:** 0	**G:** 51	**G:** 51	**G:** 204
B: 102	**B:** 102	**B:** 153	**B:** 255	**B:** 204

⑥ <CENTER>: The **<CENTER>** tag centers whatever is included in it. You would close the tag with **</CENTER>** to specify other types of alignments.

⑦ <IMG SRC>: An **<IMG SRC>** tag instructs the browser to display an image.

file name: **man.gif**   file name: **newlogo.gif**

These two images were used inside the **<IMG SRC>** tag on my home page. Both are transparent GIFs, meaning that the background colors (black and gray, respectively) dropped out on the final web page. For more information on transparency, check out Chapter 3, "Web File Formats," and Chapter 6, "Transparency."

⑧ <P>: The **<P>** tag inserts a paragraph break (single line space) between text or images.

The above example scratches only the surface of HTML. If you are interested in delving deeper into HTML, consider purchasing one of the books on page 11.

Studying other's source code is a great way to teach yourself HTML.

HTML software

No one except a die-hard programmer (and no offense to you folks at all) would want, by choice, to work with HTML. HTML stands for **H**yper**T**ext **M**arkup **L**anguage. It is the language with which web pages are written, and therefore designed, although most designers would cringe at the thought of calling HTML a design layout language.

And that's precisely the point. HTML was not written to be a design language. It was written to be a display language, with the intent that it might display differently on different machines and operating systems. Ever notice how browser software allows you to change your fonts and their sizes, and whether images and links are turned on or off? HTML was supposed to be a transportable language that could be customized to the liking of the end-user's machine.

HTML is what made the web possible, but HTML has also become known as a designer's nightmare. There has never been a design medium in the past that allowed its audience to change the content at whim. If you have ever created computer graphics before, you're used to having a sense of comfort that what you see as the final result is what everyone will see. When your graphic and layout design are finished, it can never be changed. HTML plays havoc with a designer's quest for control. It is one of the strangest design mediums ever unleashed upon us, and that is because it was never intended to be a design medium in the first place.

Many of the chapters in this book teach you how to trick HTML into obedience, but the starting point is HTML, whether you like it or not. HTML is the language of the web. Do you have to know HTML to design web pages? No, but it sure helps. Frankly, some of my favorite all-time sites were designed by artists who never touched the code. They teamed up with an HTML programmer and did what they knew best—design.

By my definition we designers are control freaks. It is in our nature to want to control how our artwork looks; that's why we are good at what we do. Most of us, in fact, are passionate about making our artwork look just exactly to our liking. Web page design is definitely full of intense challenges, and you can decide to take them on or pass the buck to a programmer.

should you learn HTML?

I think it is great to know HTML, but not in all cases. The advantage to knowing and understanding HTML is that you will be in better control of knowing what is possible and what is not. You will not have to hear no from someone else who might not care about your design as much as you do.

If you want to learn HTML, there are a few different camps to subscribe to: those who learn HTML and understand what the tags do and mean, those who use an HTML editor with automated tags, and those who use a WYSIWYG HTML editor and don't know why anything works but get finished web pages anyway. Let's examine the options.

text-based editors

I taught myself HTML using a stripped-down word processor. I wrote every tag by hand because that is how I learn new things the best. I typically learn best by doing, not reading or studying. I viewed the source of pages I liked and often copied what I liked as a starting point. I wanted to understand HTML because that is the kind of person I am. I am not representative of everybody, but this learning method fit my personality.

As an experienced teacher, I can tell you for certain that different people have different learning methods, different aptitudes, and different needs and goals. There is no one right way to learn HTML. If you really want to understand what you're doing and why, the method I used works great. It requires patience and persistence and the acceptance that you'll make mistakes and won't get instant results. The payoff is that you'll understand what you're doing and will approach this medium with a greater degree of confidence.

There are great online tutorials for learning HTML. A few of my favorites are:

- ✍ http://www.microsoft.com/workshop/design/design-contents1.htm#des

- ✍ http://help.netscape.com/links.html

- ✍ http://ncdesign.kyushu-id.ac.jp/

Another great way to learn HTML is to study other people's source code. In most popular browsers, you'll find a source view option located under the File menu. Browse the web looking for pages you like; then view the source code and learn the tricks of the trade. There's no better way.

text-based HTML editors

HTML editors are dedicated word processors that have automated tags built in. Normally, these tags are accessible via menu commands or handy toolbars. If you don't know a word of HTML, these types of editors will baffle you. So what good is an automated tag if you don't understand what tags do in the first place?

If you practice the methods described earlier of teaching yourself HTML in a standard word processor, you will come to want and appreciate a text-based HTML editor. Some of them have spell-checkers, HTML checkers (to validate, or ensure that you've written correct HTML), search-and-replace functionality, and broken-link checkers.

Most HTML editors are found on the web, and can be downloaded for free or for free trial periods. The best way to find HTML editors is on the web itself. Here are some good starting points:

- http://www.shareware.com

- http://www.yahoo.com/Computers_and_Internet/Internet/World_Wide_Web/HTML_Editors/Macintosh/

- http://www.yahoo.com/Computers_and_Internet/Internet/World_Wide_Web/HTML_Editors/MS_Windows/

Here are some reviews and comparisons of popular HTML editors that can be found online:

- http://www.cnet.com/Content/Reviews/Compare/11htmleds/

- http://www.dsport.com/sjm/resources.html

- http://www.pcmag.com/iu/features/1520/_open.htm

wysiwyg HTML editors

WYSIWYG (**W**hat**Y**ou**S**ee**I**s**W**hat**Y**ou**G**et) stands for a new breed of HTML editor that takes the pain out of writing this damn stuff. At least it seems that way. WYSIWYG editors don't require that you know a word of HTML. In fact many of them shield you from it so successfully that you may author pages and never understand or learn a word of code.

There's nothing wrong with that! I mean, how many people write their own word processing software or PostScript commands? People who like and understand how to program live for this stuff, and very few of the rest of us enjoy it much at all.

The problem is that HTML tags change all the time. New file formats and plug-ins and browser features make this a changing landscape unparalleled by typical word processing or PostScript software. Web design and development is an emerging medium, and most of us are eager guinea pigs that want to propel it further!

The only way that WYSIWYG editors could truly keep pace would be if they changed on a weekly basis. This is not to suggest that they aren't useful at all. Au contraire! They are wonderful. Anyone who has ever programmed frames or a complicated nested table will be in ecstasy letting a program do it for them without coding. I use WYSIWYG editors myself—especially when I'm in a hurry. They are fantastic time-savers and help you get your ideas out quickly without being bogged down by programming strange tags and adding opening and closing brackets and slashes everywhere.

The problem is that once you've gotten the web design bug, you'll want to try new things that the WYSIWYG editor won't support. And, if you've relied exclusively on the editor to compose pages, you won't have gotten any of the necessary skills to understand how to extend its capabilities. WYSIWYG editors often throw in their own HTML tags that certain browsers don't recognize. Or you might want to use a new plug-in or file format that they don't support yet. It's an easier, but more limited architecture.

The perfect world would be to have the browser also be the HTML editor. Every time the browser changes, the HTML editor changes too. Well—without naming names—even the most popular browser software doesn't fully support its own tags. These editors still have some growing up to do, but I'll be the first in line to endorse them once they're mature.

23

summary

This chapter has outlined some general guidelines and suggestions for getting started in web design. What follows is a summary of its main points.

- Use search engines to list your site and find reference material on the web. They are one of the web's most useful and valuable resources.

- Regardless of whether you're on a Mac or PC, you will still be able to design web pages. There are advantages and disadvantages to either platform.

- You don't need a high-speed computer to author and publish web pages; having ample disk space and RAM are much more important.

- If you have the opportunity, choose the best video and sound card you can afford. A large monitor is helpful when working with graphics software because of the many menus and windows.

- A CD-ROM drive is useful for downloading software, but high-speed drives are important only if you're planning to play games or run interactive presentations.

- Don't skimp on your modem purchase; fast is best, fastest is bestest!

- When choosing a scanner, color scanning speed should be your primary objective; resolution is less important in web design.

- If you plan to create a lot of web graphics, Photoshop is universally recognized as the leader in digital imaging.

computer screen design

Everything that is wonderful about the web—global accessibility, cross-platform compatibility, networked distribution, and ever-improving-technology—has a trade-off somewhere down the graphics creation road. On a printed page, everyone sees the same thing (with the exception of those who are visually impaired). A printed page has fixed dimensions. A printed page is designed once and forever stays the same. A printed page cannot be changed once it is finished.

Creating artwork for the web is very different from other visual delivery mediums because you're publishing your work to computer screens instead of printed pages. Computer systems vary widely. Some have small screens, some large. Some have color, some do not. Different operating systems deal with color differently. Some people have fast Internet connections, some do not. Different browsers display artwork differently. Different computer platforms have different fonts. It's the biggest design nightmare you could ever dream up—and your one chance of harnessing control over it is to understand the nature of the beast.

You can't possibly design a page that will look the same under all conditions without pandering to the lowest common denominator. That is not the route I advocate in this book. I believe that knowledge gives you power—if you arm yourself with an awareness of what can work and what can go wrong, and take whatever measures within your control to avoid the common pitfalls of this medium, your design can triumph over the obstacles.

This chapter reviews browser differences, monitor settings, and cross-platform compatibility issues, and offers an overview of bit-depth settings and gamma. These issues represent some of the common pitfalls that can plague web publishers.

Web Environment 2

browser differences

Back in the early days of web graphics, there were dozens of browsers with huge gaps in feature sets. Browsers have improved to the point now where we've emerged from the browser discrepancy era of the past to the present era of the browser wars. Competition has served web designers well. The major differences between feature sets that existed a year ago have become much less problematic.

What is a browser, and what does it do? It's software that reads web pages and displays them for you. Different browsers can interpret the visual content of a web page differently. If you are attempting to create a visually pleasing site, this means you have the maddening task of designing a presentation that is subject to change according to which browser it's viewed from.

Why do browsers interpret the pages differently? Shouldn't there be fixed standards? The browser interprets HTML (**H**yper**T**ext **M**arkup **L**anguage) code, which is the type of programming required to author web pages. HTML uses tags for including links, graphics, and other media on a web page. HTML was created as an attempt to be a universally accepted, cross-platform standard language for displaying information, text, and visuals on the web. Standards usually involve a standards committee, and committees often take a long time to agree on what they will officially support.

Officially sanctioned HTML of the old days allowed for one-color text, text that was left-justified with paragraph breaks, left-justified images, and little else. This understandably created frustration among designers and web browser developers who wanted to see the web evolve faster than the time it took outside committees to make formal decisions.

Entrepreneurial developers (primarily Netscape) took matters into their own hands and made web browsers that supported more options, without the blessings or participation of the HTML standards committee. New HTML code was developed that was supported only on proprietary browser systems, starting with Netscape and followed by others. This created outrage among some, and an outpouring of support from others who created an avalanche of web pages that included these new, unofficial HTML features.

As designers, it is not surprising that we want as many design features for the web as we can get our hands on. HTML today enables us do a lot more than it used to, and we are grateful for every small morsel of design flexibility newly thrown our way. The downside is that some of these new design options have created a more confusing web design environment.

HTML for different browsers

Most of the tags this book discusses work in the three major browsers: Netscape, Microsoft Internet Explorer (MSIE), and Mosaic. AOL's browser is the only popular browser that seriously lags behind the rest, but now that AOL will let you use other browsers, this should not be of much concern to web designers.

An invaluable resource for checking on browser discrepancies was put together by Kevin Ready, co-author of the book *Hybrid HTML Design*. You'll find a table that shows all known HTML tags and which browsers support which tags here.

✍ http://www.browserbydesign.com/
   resources/appa/apa1.htm

The book details how to design pages that are not only intended for display in all browsers, but perform optimally in each as well.

✎ **Hybrid HTML Design**
   Author: Kevin Ready and Janine Warner
   Imprint: New Riders Publishing
   ISBN: 1-56205-617-4
   Retail Price: $35.00 U.S.

You can get the latest updates about browser versions at this marvelous site created by Dave Garaffa.

✍ http://www.browserwatch.iworld.com

Here's a chart that was prepared by the BrowserWatch site, dated 02/27/97.

(Must Have .25% Share Or Better)
Printed with permission

browser types visiting browserwatch	
Netscape Navigator	46.8%
Microsoft Internet Explorer	40.6%
Unknown	1.84%
Ibrowse	1.36%
Cyberdog	1.21%
AmigaVoyager	1.11%
IBM WebExplorer	0.94%
Lynx	0.84%
NetJet	0.59%
AOL (for Windows)	1.44%
WWWC	1.42%
Amiga-A-Web	1.34%
Symantic Notify Internet Session	0.31%
FFiNet32.DLL	0.29%
PlanetWeb	0.25%

cross-platform hell!

One of the coolest things about the World Wide Web is that it's cross-platform, and people on Macs, PCs, Suns, and SGIs all get to communicate together in the same location for the first time in history.

If you're curious to know the percentage of systems used to access the web, here's the breakdown according to ✍ http://browserwatch.iworld. com/stats/stats.html.

systems used to access the web	
Windows	54.7%
Macintosh	24.3%
Unix	23.25%
OS	4.27%
Unknown	2.23%
Amiga	0.025%
WebTV	0.034%
Sega Saturn	0.025%
NeXt	0.03%
VC/CMS	0.01%

The unfortunate fact about cross-platform authoring is that viewers log on to the web by using different computers with different color spaces, color cards, monitor types, and monitor sizes. If you want to make yourself sad, spend hours creating a beautiful full-color graphic and then view it on someone's portable computer with a 4-bit color display. It's not a pretty sight. This is typical of some of the things that can happen unexpectedly to artwork that you post to your web site.

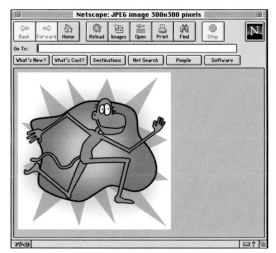

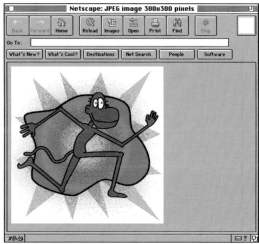

Here is an image viewed in a browser in 24-bit color.

Here's what the same image looks like on a limited color monitor (4-bit or 16-color).

What can you do about such unplanned cross-platform discrepancies? In the case of viewers looking at your site from black-and-white portables or machines intended for video games, there's not much you can do except accept that the web will never offer full control over how your site is displayed. It's both the beauty of the medium and the curse of it. However, if you decide to make a site that relies on 24-bit color and a 21" monitor, you can see by the above how much you're probably limiting your potential audience.

color calibration issues

One of the problems with color on computer screens is that few monitors are calibrated accurately to one another. Shades of a color often vary wildly from computer to computer, and from platform to platform. (If you've ever owned two television sets, you know the color from set to set can vary wildly.) Anyone who works for a company with more than one computer knows that the colors shift between systems—even between identical operating systems and identical hardware.

Color calibration is a distressing problem for web designers who expect the colors they've picked to look the same on everyone's system. Macs, PCs, SGIs, and Suns all have different color cards and monitors, and none of them are calibrated to each other.

SGI

Sun

Apple

PC

Because you now see for yourself that you have no control over the calibration of systems that your work will be viewed on, what can you do to make good-looking graphics that look good everywhere? What becomes more important than the colors you pick and what is stressed throughout this book is the contrast and value of a graphic. If you achieve contrast and value balance, then the brightness and darkness, or color differences, on various platforms are going to be less objectionable.

Does your page pass the bit-depth test? Here's my home page viewed in 8-bit color, grayscale, and black and white.

Across different computer platforms, the calibration problem is amplified by gamma differences. Gamma dictates the brightness and contrast of the computer's display. Macs, for example, are typically much brighter than PCs because of the differences in Macintosh's native gamma settings. Both calibration and gamma pose variables that are impossible to control in web design.

Although these numbers vary widely from different sources, it is generally reported that Mac and SGI monitors are close to the same settings, but PCs are much darker.

average monitor factory settings	
SGI	1.7 gamma
Mac	1.8 gamma
PC	2.5 gamma

the importance of value

What is value? Value is defined here as the display of lights and darks in an image. Value is especially important in the context of web graphics. Differences in computer platforms, gamma settings, or monitor calibrations can wreak havoc on the readability of images. A dark image created on one machine may come out black or appear tinted on another. Macintosh computers are generally lighter than Windows-based machines. Web pages can now also be viewed over television screens, which are calibrated altogether differently from computer monitors.

So how do you know if you are creating an image with values that will display properly on other machines? You can start by making sure your images have a good range from black to white. Don't place all the important information in the dark areas because they might go to black and fade out on someone's PC. And the same goes for light areas. We can't have absolute control over how someone will see our images, so making these images as readable as possible in terms of value should be your highest priority. Always view your images on other platforms to see whether your images achieve their intended values.

A great exercise is to temporarily throw your monitor into grayscale mode and then view your image to see whether its values are reading as you expected. This converts all the color data to blacks, whites, and grays. This change of settings yields much better feedback about brightness and contrast than a color display can.

Colors are notoriously deceptive when judging brightness and darkness because variables, such as a fluorescent color or subtle hand tinting, are overpowering when judging value.

Here's an example of the original image.

When viewing the image in grayscale, it almost disappears! This is because the values (lights and darks) are close together.

Here is the color-corrected version.

See how the grayscale version looks.

Personally, when working on my Mac, I try to make graphics a little lighter than I normally would, knowing that they'll display darker on PCs. When working on my PC, I do the opposite and make graphics slightly darker. There's no way to make it work perfectly everywhere, but knowing these general differences makes you an "informed" web designer so that you can make educated guesses about overall color brightness. I recommend that you always view your graphics on as many platforms as possible and make necessary changes when needed based on informed feedback.

Cross-platform authoring is possible on the web, but that doesn't necessarily mean it looks good. Take the following items into consideration, and you'll be able to make the best of a difficult design situation:

- Your pages will look different on different computer monitors and platforms.

- Check your pages on other platforms and make informed decisions for changes if necessary.

- Pay attention to the brightness and contrast of a graphic, and it will look readable, even when viewed under poor monitor conditions.

high res versus low res

Because your delivery medium is a computer screen and not a printed page, high-resolution files are not part of web design life. High-resolution graphics are intended to be printed on high-resolution printers, not displayed on standard computer monitors. A typical screen monitor's resolution is 72 dpi whereas a high-resolution image is often 300+ dpi.

For those of you who have worked with high-resolution files before, you may recall that in order to view them 1:1, you generally have to use the magnifying glass tool many times, resulting in a huge cropped image on your computer screen. The reason for this is that a computer screen can't physically display a high-resolution file. If you put a high-resolution file on the web, it can display only at 1:1 magnification, meaning that it will appear much bigger than you intended. Most likely, your goal for working in high resolution is to ensure the highest possible quality for your image, although in actuality, you would defeat that purpose.

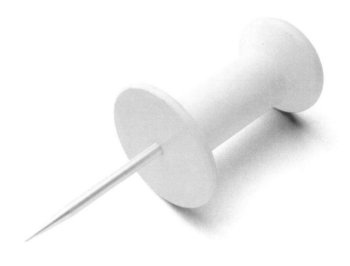

Pixels, Not Inches!

Whenever working on images for the web, set your graphics to be measured in pixels, not inches. Inches are needed when creating artwork that will be printed on paper; pixels are the standard unit of measurement for screen-based bound images.

In Photoshop, go under the Image menu and select Image Size. This shows what the resolution of the image is, which in this case is 72 dpi.

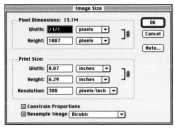

Here's the 72 dpi image in Netscape. It appears exactly the way it should look.

In this second example, the resolution is set to 300 dpi. In print graphics this would improve the appearance of this image significantly, but in web graphics it results in an image that is way too big for the screen to display.

Here's an example of the 300 dpi image displayed in Netscape. Get the picture?

bit depth for images

Uh-oh, the dreaded bit-depth subject! For those math-phobic people, this topic will most likely sound intimidating. Bit depth is extremely important in understanding web graphics. Bit depth can refer to the number of colors in an image or the number of colors a computer system is capable of displaying.

bit depth

32-bit	16.7+ million colors plus an 8-bit (256-level) grayscale mask
24-bit	16.7+ million colors
16-bit	65.5 thousand colors
15-bit	32.8 thousand colors
8-bit	256 colors
7-bit	128 colors
6-bit	64 colors
5-bit	32 colors
4-bit	16 colors
3-bit	8 colors
2-bit	4 colors
1-bit	2 colors

Here's a visual guide to refer to whenever you need it.

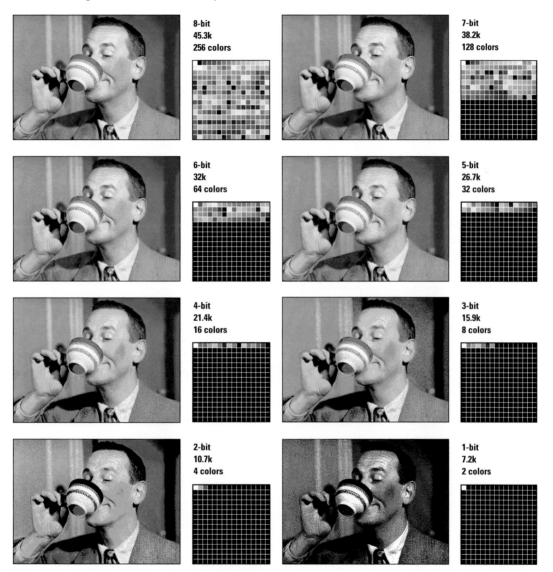

8-bit
45.3k
256 colors

7-bit
38.2k
128 colors

6-bit
32k
64 colors

5-bit
26.7k
32 colors

4-bit
21.4k
16 colors

3-bit
15.9k
8 colors

2-bit
10.7k
4 colors

1-bit
7.2k
2 colors

Notice the lower the bit depth, the lower the quality and the lower the file size becomes? You will find much more information about how to choose which bit depth to use for your web graphics in Chapter 4, "Speedy Web Graphics."

bit depth for monitors

So far, bit depth has been defined as it relates to images. There are actually two instances where understanding bit depth is important. The first is to understand the bit depth of an image, and the second is to understand the bit depth of your end viewer's monitor. In this section, let's look at the monitor's bit depth, not the bit depth of images.

Most professional digital artists have 24-bit monitors (which can display up to 16.7 million colors). The average computer user—hence the average member of your web-viewing audience—has an 8-bit (256-color) monitor. This makes sense if you think about it because the majority of computer monitors are owned by average people who bought the least expensive version of their computer system, not professional graphic artists who might have greatly enhanced systems.

Herein lies a huge problem. The majority of people who create artwork for web sites are viewing the artwork under better conditions than the average end user. This makes for a communication gap—one this book hopes to bridge rather than skim over, or worse, ignore.

If a computer system has only an 8-bit color card, it cannot physically view more than 256 colors at once. When people with 256-color systems view your web screens, they cannot see images in 24-bit, even if they want to. They can't prevent it, and neither can you. Specific advice for working with 8-bit color and files are provided in Chapter 4, "Speedy Web Graphics," and Chapter 5, "Cross-Platform Color."

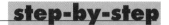

step-by-step

Changing Your Monitor's Bit Depth

☞ **1**   Always run a bit-depth preview test on your web pages before you send them out for the world to see. Change your monitor settings to 256 colors, and you'll see how your artwork translates under those conditions.

☞ **2**   Instructions follow on how to change your monitor to display in 256 colors so that you can preview the bad news before others do.

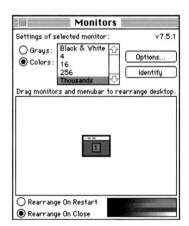

Windows 3.1: From Program Manager, display the Change System Settings dialog box by double-clicking on the Windows Setup icon (generally found in the Main program group) and choosing Change System Settings from the Options menu.

Macintosh: Open the control panel called "Monitors" or "Sights and Sound." (Control panel items are in your System Folder.)

Windows 95: Access your display properties by using your right mouse button and selecting Display properties.

summary

The web environment is different from other computer graphics mediums. It is screen-based, where most other digital graphics disciplines are print- or film-based. Understanding how to work with artwork for computer screen delivery, with cross-platform compatibility in mind, is the key to creating successful web graphics. This chapter's main points are summarized as follows:

- Browser and platform differences can affect the way your pages display. Be sure to check your finished work in Netscape and Internet Explorer, and on PCs and Macs, whenever possible.

- Viewers log onto the web using different computers with different color spaces, color cards, monitor types, and monitor sizes. Make sure your site reads well on standard size monitors with 256-color video cards, by changing the resolution of your own setup in order to preview its appearance.

- Pay careful attention to the value (contrast and brightness) of your images. PC, Mac, Sun, and SGI all have different color and brightness calibrations. If you make sure your images have good contrast (that is, light text against dark background or vice-versa), your web page will hold up well under the various conditions from which it will be viewed.

- Always create web images at 72 dpi, using RGB color space.

- Preview your pages in 256 colors. Most end users will have limited color displays.

compression

It's impossible to discuss web graphics file formats without discussing compression. Compression is not a necessary feature in other computer graphic file format specifications, which is why the file formats you'll find on the web might be new to you. Web-based image file formats have to implement impressive compression schemes in order to transform large images to small file sizes. Unfortunately, at times, with compression comes loss of quality.

Some web file formats use lossy compression techniques, meaning that there will be some loss of quality to the resulting images. Don't let that scare you though; there is no way these file formats could impose the required amount of compression needed for web delivery and not sacrifice some quality. Remember once again, print quality is not expected on the web.

The two types of image file formats most commonly accepted by graphic web browsers are JPEGs and GIFs. One difference between them is that JPEGs can be 24-bit (include up to 16.7 million colors) and GIFs must be 8-bit or less (256 colors maximum).

JPEG stands for **J**oint **P**hotographic **E**xperts **G**roup, and GIF stands for **G**raphic **I**nter-change **F**ormat. These names tell you, in each respective acronym, which format is best for which kind of image. JPEGs were designed to compress photographs, and GIFs were designed to compress graphics.

There will be times when you will want to make a photograph into a GIF, such as with transparent GIFs and animated GIFs, and times when you want to make a graphic into a JPEG, such as when a logo or graphic is combined with a photograph. This chapter will help you answer which file format to use when and why.

It's easy to convert to JPEGs and GIFs from other image file formats, such as PICT, BMP, TGA, TIFF, or EPS, if you have the proper software, such as Photoshop or Photo-Paint. As well, many imaging programs support the capability to save or resave your graphics as JPEGs and GIFs.

This section examines the pros and cons of web-based image file formats and gives you an understanding of how to choose which file format is appropriate for specific styles of artwork. The next chapter, Chapter 4, "Speedy Web Graphics," offers step-by-step instruction and tips on how to create the smallest possible GIFs and JPEGs by using Photoshop and other imaging tools.

Web File Formats 3

GIF compression

Unlike most other computer graphic file formats, GIF (**G**raphic **I**nter-change **F**ormat) was designed specifically for online delivery because it was originally developed for CompuServe in the late 1980s. The file format compresses graphics beautifully but can also be used for photographic images. Whenever you create graphics, such as logos, illustrations, or cartoons, the GIF file format is recommended.

GIF uses a compression scheme called LZW, which is based on work done by Lempel-Ziv & Welch. The patent for LZW compression is owned by a company called Unisys, which charges developers such as Net-scape and Photoshop licensing and royalty fees for selling products that use the GIF file format. End users, such as ourselves (web publishers) and our audience (web visitors), do not have to pay licensing fees or worry about any of this. There is some speculation that the GIF file for-mat may be less prevalent at some point because of the fees, but we hope not. GIFs are accepted by all browsers, GIFs are small, and GIFs do things that many other file formats do not, such as animation, trans-parency, and interlacing.

The GIF file format, by definition, can contain only 256 colors (8-bit) or less. This is not the case with JPEGs, which by definition contain millions of colors (24-bit). Because GIFs are an indexed-color file format (256 colors or less), it's extremely beneficial to have a thorough understand-ing of bit-depth settings and palette management when preparing GIF images.

There are two different flavors of GIF: GIF87a and GIF89a. Don't worry about memorizing these numbers; you'll rarely need to address the file format by its formal name. GIF87a supports transparency and interlacing, whereas GIF89a supports transparency, interlacing, and animation (more information on these features follows). As of this book's printing, the major browsers (Netscape, MSIE, and Mosaic) all support both GIF format specifications. You don't really have to refer to the names GIF87a or GIF89a unless you want to sound techie. Most of us simply call these files by the features used, be it a transparent GIF, animated GIF, or plain vanilla GIF.

GIF compression is lossless, meaning that the GIF compression algorithm will not cause any unwanted image degradation. The process of converting a 24-bit image to 256 or fewer colors will cause image degradation on its own, however, so don't get too excited yet!

Pronunciation

First of all, how is GIF pronounced? Some people say it with a soft g as in jiffy, and some with a hard g as in gift. I once took a poll in which the hard g pronunciation won, but old-timer CompuServe subscribers, where the file format first appeared, swear it's pronounced with a soft g. In my classes and lectures, I alternate the pronunciation, and think it's funny that no one agrees.

GIFs for photographic imagery

GIFs are definitely designed to handle graphics better than photographs. But that doesn't mean that there won't be times where you have to turn photographs into GIFs anyway. You may want to use transparency or animation, which are two features that JPEGs do not offer.

GIFs can be saved at any bit depth from 8-bit down to 1-bit. The bit depth refers to how many colors the image contains. Generally, the lower the bit depth, the smaller the GIF.

24-bit • original PICT • 176k

8-bit • 44.2k   7-bit • 37.6k   6-bit • 32.8k   5-bit • 29.3k

4-bit • 22.9k   3-bit • 18.8k   2-bit • 13.2k   1-bit • 11.2k

Your job when preparing a GIF is to take it down to its lowest bit-depth level and still maintain acceptable image quality. Depending on how important this image is, acceptable quality falls somewhere between 6-bit and 4-bit, which offers a 20–50% file size reduction over the 8-bit version.

GIFs for illustration-style imagery

GIFs work much better for graphics than photographs. Graphics are defined here as illustrations, cartoons, or logos. Such graphics typically use areas of solid color, and GIFs handle compression of solid color better than the varied colors found in photographs. Because the GIF file format is lossless, illustrations with limited colors (less than 256) won't lose any quality. Because JPEG is a lossy method, it actually introduces image artifacts into solid color.

A GIF file is lossless, meaning that no loss of quality is obtained during the conversion process.

A JPEG is a lossy compression method, meaning that the conversion process will create a loss in quality. When JPEGs are used on illustration-based artwork, unwanted artifacts appear.

interlaced GIFs

If you've toured the web much, you've encountered interlaced GIFs. They're those images that start out blocky, and appear less and less blocky until they come into full focus.

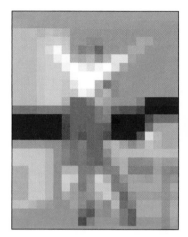  

These examples simulate the effect of interlacing on a browser. The image starts chunky and comes into focus over time. This allows the end viewer to decide whether to wait for your graphic to finish or click onward.

Interlacing doesn't affect the overall size or speed of a GIF. In theory, interlacing is supposed to make it possible for your end viewer to get a rough idea of your visuals, and to make a decision whether to wait or click onward before the image finishes rendering. Again—in theory—interlacing is supposed to save time. Unfortunately for the end viewer, being forced to wait for the entire image to finish coming into focus to read essential information is often a frustrating experience. In other words, interlaced images save time only if you don't have to wait for them to finish.

My recommendation is that you do not use interlaced GIFs for important visual information that is critical to viewing your site. An imagemap or navigation icon, for example, must be seen in order to fulfill its function. Although interlaced GIFs serve their purpose on nonessential graphics, they only frustrate end users when used on essential graphics.

transparent GIFs

Transparent GIFs are used to create the illusion of irregularly shaped artwork. All computer-made images end up in rectangular-shaped files; it's the nature of the medium. Certain file formats, such as GIF, can store masked regions, which create the illusion of shapes other than rectangles. This "masked region" appears to be transparent.

For example, you could create a red circle inside a blue square. Then, by instructing the blue background color of the circle to disappear, or be transparent, the red circle will appear to be free floating over another image. Transparency works by creating masked regions that are instructed to disappear when combined with other files.

Here's an example of artwork from Lynda's Homegurrrl site that has been defined to be transparent. The gray color was instructed to drop out within transparency software. Precise instructions for creating transparent artwork are found in Chapter 6, "Transparency."

Transparency comes in two forms: 8-bit transparency and 1-bit transparency. 8-bit transparency is the best, but it isn't supported by GIFs or by web browsers. 8-bit transparency is what is used by the file formats Photoshop, TGA, and PICT. 8-bit transparency is also called alpha channel-based transparency, and can support up to 256 different levels of opacity (which is why it looks so great!). GIFs support 1-bit transparency, which makes it a much more limited type of masking.

This screen shows the transparent artwork in context. Once the GIF transparency is recognized within browser software, the browser allows the rectangular artwork to appear irregularly shaped.

This image represents the type of compositing you can do in Photoshop and 8-bit transparency, where it can easily display differing levels of transparency, glows, and blurs. GIF transparency is unfortunately much more crude than this.

note

PNG Transparency

The only type of web file format that supports 8-bit transparency is PNG, which was not widely implemented at the time this chapter was written. If you are interested in more information about PNG, try ✍ http://quest.jpl.nasa.gov/PNG/png.html. GIF is much more common than PNG, and is supported by far more browsers, so it is still much more practical to get your GIF-making chops up to speed and make the best of what it offers.

animated GIFs

Animated GIFs are part of the GIF89a specification. They are formally called multiblock GIFs because multiple images can be stored as separate blocks within a single GIF document. When the GIF document is viewed, the multiple images display, one at a time, and produce streaming animation.

Streaming is a wonderfully appropriate method for displaying animation over the web. Streaming means that each frame of the animation displays one after the other, so that your end user doesn't have to wait for the entire file to download before seeing anything. Other animation formats in the past required that the entire movie download before a single frame could be viewed.

Animated GIFs function much like automated slide shows. They can include custom palette information and be set to play at different speeds. They can include interlacing and transparency, too! The beauty of animated GIFs is that they require no plug-ins, and the authoring tools to create them are often free and easy to learn. As well, major browsers (Netscape, Internet Explorer, and Mosaic) support them, so you can include them in web pages without worrying about compatibility or accessibility. Specific instruction on how to create animated GIFs and apply custom palettes is available in Chapter 12, "Animation."

Just like other GIF files, the number of colors and amount of noise in the frames affect the overall file size. If you have a 100-frame animation with each frame totaling 5k, your animated GIF will be 500k. It simply multiplies in size according to how many frames you create and the file size of the individual frame of artwork. On the other hand, your end viewer is really waiting for only 5k servings at a time, so it's nothing like the painful waiting that a standard 500k GIF would incur!

Two popular GIF animation authoring tools are:

Microsoft's GIF Animator
http://www.microsoft.com/imagecomposer/gifanimator/gifanin.htm

GIFBuilder/freeware (Mac)
http://iawww.epfl.ch/Staff/Yves.Piguet/clip2gif-home/GifBuilder.html

Some good animated GIF references:

Royal Frazier's awesome site
http://member.aol.com/roalef/gifanim.htm

GIFBuilder's FAQ
http://iawww.epfl.ch/Staff/Yves.Piguet/clip2gif-home/GifBuilderDoc/GifBuilder-FAQs.html

Microsoft's Animated GIF FAQ
http://www.microsoft.com/imagecomposer/gifanimator/gafaq.htm

Here's a 30-frame animation, found on Lynda's Homegurrrl site at ✍ http://www.lynda.com/anim.html. It's hard to tell the subtle changes from frame to frame when viewed in sequence, but once the frames are played in motion over time, the '50s man appears to be bobbing his head, waving his finger, and has little lines flowing out of the side of his head. The entire animation totals 64k in size. Why? It's only two colors, with no anti-aliasing.

JPEG

The JPEG (pronounced jay-peg) file format offers a 24-bit alternative to the 8-bit GIF file format. This is especially great for photographic content because 24-bit photographs do not dither! (Check out Chapter 2, "Web Environment," and Chapter 5, "Cross-Platform Color," for more information on dithering.) One added advantage to dealing with JPEGs is that they don't need you to define the palette for them, like GIFs. Whenever an image format includes millions of colors (24-bit), palette and color mapping issues disappear. This is because enough colors are allowed to rely on the original image's color information, and substitute colors are no longer necessary.

JPEG was developed specifically for photographic-style images. It looks to areas with subtle tonal and color changes and offers the best compression when it encounters that type of imagery. GIF doesn't handle this type of image well at all, in terms of quality or file size!

JPEG compresses this type of image beautifully, and offers the best compression as well—this image is 21.1k.

GIF does not compress this type of image well, and it creates unwanted dithering (pixelization). It doesn't compress photographs well either—this image is more than twice as big as the JPEG, at 47.9k.

JPEG is a lossy compression algorithm, meaning that it removes information from your image and, therefore, causes a loss in quality. JPEG does a great job of doing this, so the difference in information data is often not visible or objectionable. It does introduce arti-facts in some instances, especially where it encounters solid colors. This is a by-product of its lossy compression methods.

Unlike the GIF file format, JPEGs require both compression and decompression. This means that JPEG files need to decompress when they're viewed. Even though a GIF and a JPEG might be identical sizes, or sometimes even when the JPEG is smaller, the JPEG might take longer to download or view from a web browser because of the added time required to decompress.

Another difference between GIF and JPEG is the fact that you can save JPEGs in a variety of compression levels. This means that more or less compression can be applied to an image, depending on which looks best.

The examples on the next page were taken from Photoshop. Photoshop employs the JPEG compression settings of max, high, medium, and low. In Photoshop, these terms relate to quality, not the amount of compression.

Although there are good reasons for saving photographs as GIF (animation, transparency, and interlacing), there are no good reasons for saving graphics as JPEGs, unless the graphics are combined with photographs. With photographic content in general, don't be afraid to try low-quality settings; the file size saving is usually substantial, and the quality penalties are not too steep.

max   **high**   **med**   **low**

46.0k   35.0k   28.8k   25.8k

33.7k   25.9k   21.1k   19.0k

31.0k   24.7k   20.4k   18.6k

You can see by this test that there's not a whole lot of difference between low-quality and high-quality JPEGs, except with graphics. As we've said, leave graphics for GIF and photographs for JPEGs.

progressive JPEGs versus standard

Progressive JPEGs are a new entrée into our web graphics file format vocabulary. This type of JPEG boasts much higher compression rates than regular JPEG and supports interlacing (where the graphic starts chunky and comes into focus). They were initially introduced by Netscape and are now additionally supported by MSIE and Mosaic. Progressive-JPEG-making tools for Mac and PCs are listed at ✍ http://www.in-touch.com/ pjpeg2.html#software.

Pro-JPEGs boast superior compression to regular JPEGs. They also support interlacing, much like interlaced GIFs. The only potential problem with them is older browsers will give you a broken image icon, instead of a regular JPEG. That's a steep penalty—you might want to consider whether the file savings is worth the risk.

Progressive JPEGs

max

32.9k

high

25.6k

med

20.8k

low

18.9k

JPEGs

33.7k

25.9k

21.1k

19.0k

naming images	
GIF	.gif
Interlaced GIF	.gif
Transparent GIF	.gif
Animated GIF	.gif
JPEG	.jpg
Progressive JPEG	.jpg

HTML for images

Regardless of whether you're using a regular GIF, animated GIF, transparent GIF, interlaced GIF, JPEG, or progressive JPEG format, you'll use HTML to embed the images in your web pages. More HTML instruction is offered in later chapters, but this handy chart to your left will help you understand how to name and code your web images.

✎ To insert a graphic into an HTML page, use this tag:

```
<IMG SRC="myimage.gif">
```

✎ To link an image to another image or HTML page, use this tag:

```
<A HREF="www.destination_url.com"><IMG
SRC="myimag.jpg"></A>
```

✎ To get rid of the border of an image that has been linked, do this:

```
<A HREF="www.destination_url.com"><IMG SRC="myimag.jpg"
BORDER=0></A>
```

The HTML is the easy part—it's understanding how to optimize graphics, choosing which file format for which type of image, and making the images and content that will be much harder to master!

Naming Conventions for JPEGs and GIFs

When saving a JPEG or GIF file for a web page, always use the three-letter extension of either .jpg or .gif at the end of your file name. Because many servers that store web graphics are Unix-based, it is important to pay close attention to whether your files are named with upper- or lowercase titles. The HTML document must exactly match the upper- or lowercase structure of the file name. For example, if you have something saved as "image.jpg" on your server, and your HTML reads "image.JPG", the file will not load!

summary

The thing that all web file formats have in common is compression. Understanding which type of compression is appropriate for which type of imagery will affect file size (download-ing speed) and image quality. The main points in this chapter are summarized as follows:

✎ JPEG stands for Joint Photographic Experts Group, and GIF stands for Graphic Interchange Format. These names tell you, in each respective acronym, which format is best for which kind of image. JPEGs were designed to compress pho-tographs; GIFs were designed to compress graphics.

✎ Sometimes you'll need to create photographic images as GIFs, such as when creat-ing GIF animation or transparent GIFs.

✎ GIF is a lossless compression method, meaning that it does not throw away any information from your graphics. Unfortunately, it is an 8-bit file format, which in itself can lower the quality of images.

✎ Interlaced GIFs should not be used for key navigational graphics.

✎ JPEG is a lossy compression method, meaning that it sacrifices some of the infor-mation the graphic contains to perform its file reduction. This can introduce unwanted artifacts and imperfections in certain images.

✎ Progressive JPEGs compress better than the standard, baseline JPEG, but they are not supported by all browsers. The trade-off is that end users logging onto your site with older browsers will get broken picture icons.

✎ When naming images, make sure that you use three-letter acronyms for JPEGs and GIFs, and that you check to see that upper- and lowercase lettering is consistent between your HTML and your file names.

low-bandwidth graphics

There's never before been a design medium where speed was an important judgment factor. No one looks through a magazine and says, "Oh, this image was only 90mb; and look, this one was just 5mb!" On the web, unlike other design mediums, file size makes it impossible to see the artwork if it's too big. The truth with web graphics is that an image can be stunning and communicate critical information, but if it's too big, your audience will never wait around long enough to see it. Making images speedy means learning how to make small file sizes, and that's precisely what this chapter teaches.

This chapter walks you through the stages of making smaller images, not in dimensions but in file size. You'll learn how to "read" the file size of a graphic, understand what the file format is doing to an image, and which file formats to use on which types of images. In the end, you should have a much better sense of how to create the smallest possible images for web delivery.

Speedy Web Graphics

4

your true file size

A new web vocabulary will include measuring web images by kilobytes, or kb from now on. For those who like number crunching, a kilobyte is composed of 1,024 bytes; a megabyte is composed of 1,048,576 bytes; and a gigabyte has 1,073,741,824 bytes. Files measuring in the megabytes and gigabytes will not be allowed on well-designed web pages—they take too long to view! Because of this, you'll often get the directive from a client to keep page sizes within a certain file size limit. Or you might have an internal goal of not exceeding 30kb per page. It's necessary to understand how to read the file size of a document if you're trying to make it fall within a certain target range of acceptability.

Making graphics and images that work on the web requires that images have as small a file size as possible. Understanding how compression affects image size and what types of file formats are appropriate for images is key to responsible web design.

How can you tell how many kilobytes an image is? Most Photoshop users think the readout in the lower left corner of a document informs them about the file size. Not true! These numbers relate to the amount of RAM Photoshop is allocating to your image and its scratch disk virtual memory scheme.

You also might look to your hard drive for the file size. Notice that the file size numbers are all nicely rounded figures: 11k, 33k, and 132k. Your computer rounds up the size of a file to the next largest number depending on how large your hard drive partition is. Have you ever had a file read two different file sizes on a hard drive and a floppy? That's because the computer rounds off the size of the file depending on what size storage media its on.

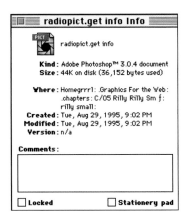

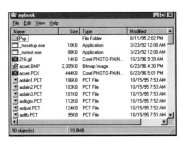

On a Mac the only way to get information about the true byte size of a file is to do a Get Info command. First, highlight the file you want to check in the Finder, go to the File menu, and then choose Get Info.

Using Win95, the file size shown in the folder directory is close to the actual file size; it will round off to the next lowest number.

To get the most accurate reading, click the file using the right mouse button, and select properties. You'll see the actual bytes.

61

how small is small?

So you know images have to be small on the web, but how small is small? Digital print designers commonly work on images ranging from tens to hundreds of megabytes as a daily fact of life. Even if you aren't working in graphics or print, you've been hearing that web graphics have to be small—but again, how small is small? A handy rule of thumb is to consider that the average person viewing the web is on a 14.4 modem, and you can expect it to take one second per kilobyte for an image to transfer. This means that a 60kb file would take one minute to download, and a 10mb file could take almost three hours!

So how do you translate your many-megabyte-sized file down to something small enough to fit on an average floppy disk? The two file formats of the web, GIF and JPEG, both offer impressive compression schemes. Saving in these formats, as long as your images are under 640×480 pixels at 72 dpi in RGB, will make fitting them on a floppy disk easy regardless of how complex your graphic is. Even though fitting a large graphic on a floppy may seem like a giant accomplishment if you're used to large files, this file size still won't cut it for the web.

To Icon or Not to Icon

Photoshop typically saves images with an icon. The icon is a small, visual representation of what the image looks like, which the file references. Photoshop icons take up a little extra room on your hard drive. This ultimately won't matter because when you send the files to your server, you'll transmit them as raw data, which will strip off the icon anyway. But if your goal is to get a more accurate reading of the true file size, you should set your preferences in Photoshop to not save an icon.

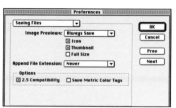

To set your preferences to not save the icon, choose File, Preferences, General. In the General dialog box, set the Image Previews to Ask When Saving.

preparing web graphics

making small GIFs

The GIF file-compression algorithm offers impressive file size reduction, but the degree of file size savings has a lot to do with how you create your GIF images. Understanding how GIFs compress is the first step in this process.

LZW compression looks to patterns of data. Whenever it encounters areas in an image that do not have changes, it can implement much higher compression. This is similar to another type of compression called run-length compression (used in BMP, TIFF, and PCX formats), but LZW writes, stores, and retrieves its code a little differently. Similar to many types of run-length compression, however, GIF compression searches for changes along a horizontal axis, and whenever it finds a new color, adds to the file size.

Here's an original image saved as a GIF that contains horizontal lines. It is 6.7k.

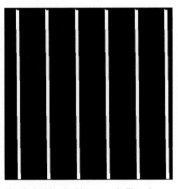

Here's the identical image, only flipped on its side so that the lines are vertical. It's a whopping 42% bigger at 11.5k!

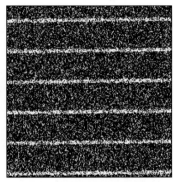

Try adding noise to the original. You'll be adding 88% to the file size. This one is 56k!

So what does the line test really teach? That artwork that has horizontal changes compresses better than artwork that doesn't. That anything with noise will more than quadruple your image's file size. That large areas of flat color compress well, and that complicated line work or dithering does not.

anti-aliasing versus aliasing

Aside from the visual complexity of the image, there are two additional factors that affect file size: bit depth and dithering methods. With all GIFs, the fewer colors (lower bit depth), the smaller the resulting file. You should remember this fact when considering whether to improve image quality through anti-aliasing.

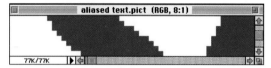

Here's an example of aliased text. It resulted in a file that totaled 3.8k when saved as a GIF.

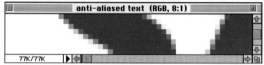

Here's an example of anti-aliased text. It resulted in a file that's 5k as a GIF. The anti-aliasing caused the file to be 24% larger!

Close-up view: Aliasing does not disguise the jaggy nature of pixel-based artwork.

Close-up view: This close-up shows how anti-aliasing creates a blended edge. This blending disguises the square-pixel-based nature of computer artwork.

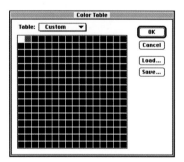

The aliased artwork used only 4 colors.

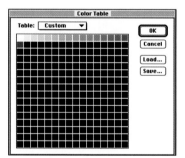

The anti-aliased artwork used 18 colors.

It's often assumed that artwork will always look better if it has anti-aliased edges. This is simply not true! Artists have never had to factor size of files into their design considerations before. Having something load 24% faster is nothing to balk at. In many cases, aliased artwork looks just as good as anti-aliased artwork, and choosing between the two approaches is something that web designers should consider whenever possible.

As well as considering whether to use aliased or anti-aliased graphics, you should also always work with browser-safe colors when creating illustration-based artwork for the web. Examples of how browser-safe colors improve the quality of illustrations are demonstrated in Chapter 5, "Cross-Platform Color."

Artwork by Yuryeong Park for the Hot Hot Hot site, ✍ http://www. hothothot.com. The entire site is done in aliased graphics, and no page exceeds 30k, even though all of the pages have several images.

Here's an example of a 700×1134 pixel GIF file created by Bruce Heavin that totals only 7.1k! Why? Lots of solid color and no anti-aliasing. This image has only 4 colors.

A background tile, previewed in Photoshop, created by Don Barnett. The source tile is only 1.7k. The savings from aliased graphics can really add up!

dithering and banding

When an image with millions of colors is converted to an image with 256 colors or less, image quality is lost. Basically, when colors are removed from the image, some sacrifices have to be made. This can take place in two forms: dithering or banding. Here are some definitions to remember:

- Dithering is the positioning of different colored pixels within an image that uses a 256-color palette to simulate a color that does not exist in the palette. A dithered image often looks noisy, or composed of scattered pixels.

- Adaptive palettes are used to convert the image to 256 colors based on existing colors within the image. Generally, adaptive dithering looks the best of all dithering methods.

- Screen dithering is what happens when a 24-bit or 16-bit image is viewed on a computer with a 256-color card. The image's color is reduced to 256 colors, and the "dither" looks uniform, as if a pattern was used.

- Banding is a process of reducing colors to 256 or less without dithering. It produces areas of solid color and generates a posterized effect.

Understanding the terminology of dithering and banding is important in web design, as these are often effects that are undesirable. Bringing down the quality of images is necessary at times for speed considerations, but riding the line between low file size and good enough quality means that you will often encounter unwanted results. These new terms help define the problems you'll encounter when creating web graphics and will be used throughout the rest of the book.

Screen dithering takes the form of a repeated pattern and creates a moiré appearance.

The dots within a "screen-dithered" image look uniform, based upon the generalized screen pattern.

This is an example of "image dithering" using an adaptive palette. It will typically look a lot better than "screen dithering" because the dither pattern is based on the content of the image, not a preset screen.

Even though the image is composed of pixellated dots, they are less obvious and objectionable because there's no obvious pattern or screen.

The banding in this image is obvious. It looks like a posterization effect.

Here's a close-up of the banding. Instead of the dots you'll find in dithering methods, the computer takes the image and breaks it into regions of solid color.

controlling color mapping

Color mapping refers to the colors that are assigned to a GIF image, and can either be taken from either the image or a predetermined palette of colors. Photoshop calls palettes that are derived from existing colors adaptive palettes. It enables you to apply external palettes (system or browser-safe, are two examples) or makes a best-guess palette (adaptive) based on the content of your image. While the numbers of colors in an image (bit-depth) affect the size of the graphic, the palette additionally affects the quality of your image. If you understand how, you can be in charge of which colors you map your images with and have more control over the resulting quality.

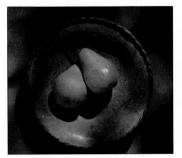  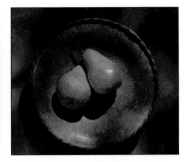

The adaptive palette looks the best because the colors are based on the content of the image. Paint Shop Pro calls this type of palette a Nearest Color palette. Photoshop calls it an adaptive palette.

The system palette image looks much worse. Even though it has the same number of colors as the adaptive palette, the colors are unrelated to the image and detract from the quality.

The browser-safe palette looks worst of all. Not only does it use fewer colors, but just like the system palette, the colors are unrelated to the image.

It's clear that an adaptive or nearest color palette gives the best results to the image, but what about when it's seen in a browser? The examples below show the results. For techniques required to assign color maps to images, check out Chapter 5, "Cross-Platform Color."

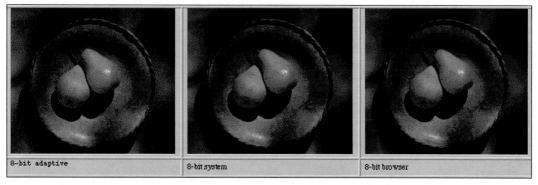

This example demonstrates how the images display in an 8-bit web browser. See any differences? The differences are minor, if any, aren't they? This is what visitors to your site would see if they had only an 8-bit display.

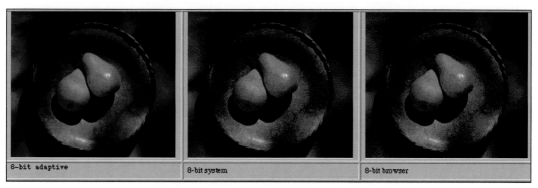

This example demonstrates how the images display in a 24-bit web browser. The adaptive GIF looks the best, does it not? The moral of the story? Use adaptive palettes for photographs saved as GIFs and let the 8-bit browsers out there remap your colors on-the-fly for you. This allows your 24-bit viewing audience to see these images at their best, and your 8-bit viewing audience is none the worse off.

photoshop's indexed color dialog box

The Indexed Color dialog box has three important functions: setting the **color depth**, the **palette**, and the **dither**. The **resolution** affects the bit depth of the image, the **palette** sets which colors are used, and the **dither** tells the program which color reduction method to use—dithering, screen, or no dithering.

How To Set Color Depth

When you convert from RGB to Indexed Color mode, you are presented with the dialog box on the left. Color depth determines how many colors are assigned to the image.

8-bit • 55.4k

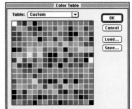

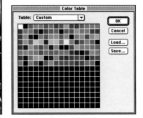

7-bit • 47.5k

6-bit • 39.7k

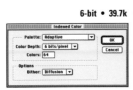

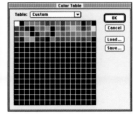

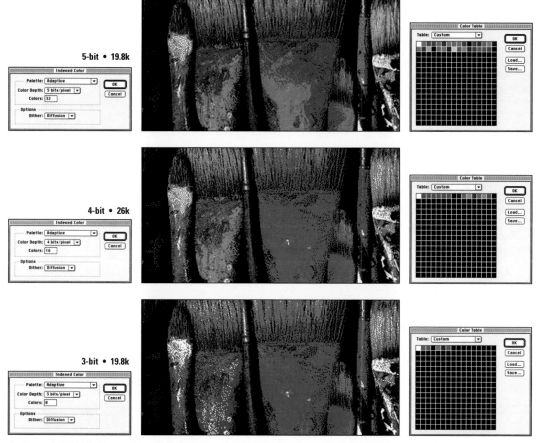

As Chapter 3, "Web File Formats," described, the factors of palette, color depth, and dither all play an important role in creating optimized (small in file size) web images. In order to implement your knowledge about file size savings, it's necessary to understand how to specify palette, color depth, and dither settings in Photoshop.

How to Set Palettes

In the Indexed Color dialog, you can also set palettes. Here are the possibilities and their effects.

• **Adaptive** •
An Adaptive palette is created from 256 colors found within the image • **55.4k**

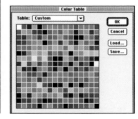

• **Custom** •
Custom allows you to load a palette of your choosing • **48.3k**

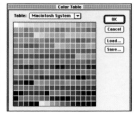

• **Exact** •
An Exact palette uses the exact colors found within the image

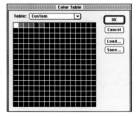

• **Previous** •
Previous uses the palette from the last conversion

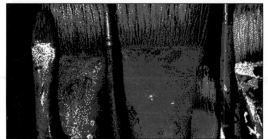

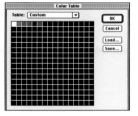

72

• **Mac System** •
Uses the Macintosh's system
palette • 48.3k

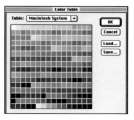

• **Windows Palette** •
Uses the Windows system
palette • 44.7k

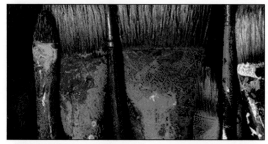

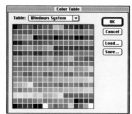

• **Uniform** •
Creates a mathematical palette based upon RGB pixel
values • 44.3k

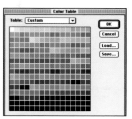

• **Web** •
Creates a palette based on
the browser-safe 216 color
cube • 42k

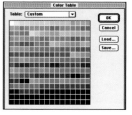

How To Set Dither Options

 In Photoshop, in order to choose to dither or not to dither, you must enter the information in the Indexed Color dialog box, which is located under the Image, Mode, Indexed Color menu. Once the Indexed Color dialog appears, the Dither setting is located under the Options setting.

Dither Diffusion establishes a dither in the image.

Dither None avoids dithering altogether but sometimes creates unwanted banding.

to dither or not to dither?

Dithering methods play a huge role in creating smaller GIFs. Any type of "noise" introduces added file size. Unfortunately, whenever you're working with photographic-based GIFs, dithering of one type or another must be employed to reduce the 24-bit color file to the 8-bit or lower bit-depth threshold of GIF.

GIF saved with dithering • 38.3k   **Photoshop's Dither None • 32.3k**   **GIF saved with dithering • 40.0k**   **Without dithering • 32.4**

There's almost no objectionable difference between these two images, regardless of whether a dithering method is used to convert to 8-bit color or Photoshop's Dither None method was chosen. Why? This image has a lot of solid areas of color to begin with. The file savings between 38.3k and 32.3k is not huge either, but the non-dither method will still yield a smaller file size.

In this example, the GIF that did not use dithering is once again smaller. The only problem is that it looks awful! Sometimes file savings does not warrant loss of quality. Whenever a photograph contains glows, feathered edges, or subtle gradations, you will have to use dithering when converting from 24-bit to 8-bit in order to maintain the image's quality.

Instructions for how to set up dither and no-dither methods for Photoshop, Paint Shop Pro, and Photo-Paint are described later in this chapter. All three programs offer the capability to set "dithering" or "no dithering."

To summarize, in order to make smaller GIFs, you should:

- Try to save the file at the lowest possible bit depth while monitoring quality.

- Try to avoid dithering, if the image can withstand it.

There is never one pat answer for making the smallest possible GIFs. Choices between bit depth and dithering methods should always be based on the image's content. In general, images with subtle gradations will need to be dithered. Images with areas of solid color will look fine without dithering.

making small JPEGs

Another difference between GIF and JPEG is the fact that you can save JPEGs in a variety of compression levels. This means that more or less compression can be applied to an image, depending on which looks best.

The following examples were taken from Photoshop. Photoshop employs the JPEG compression settings of max, high, medium, and low. In Photoshop, these terms relate to quality, not the amount of compression.

You can see by this test that there's not a whole lot of difference between low quality and high quality, except with graphics. As previously stated, leave graphics for GIF and photographs for JPEGs. Although there are good reasons for saving photographs as GIF (animation, transparency, and interlacing), there are no good reasons for saving graphics as JPEGs, unless the graphics are combined with photographs. With photographic content in general, don't be afraid to try low-quality settings; the file size savings, is usually substantial, and the quality penalties are not too steep.

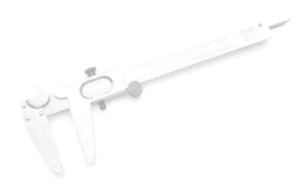

max	high	med	low

32.9k	25.6k	20.8k	18.9k
44.6k	34.2k	28.2k	25.4k
29.9k	23.9k	20.0k	18.3k

image compression charts

The next time someone asks you, "Which is better, GIF or JPEG?" you can answer confidently that there is no one method of compression that is better than another. Different types of compression are meant to work with different, specific kinds of images. Creating the absolute smallest image you can requires that you understand the differences between images and the differences between compression methods.

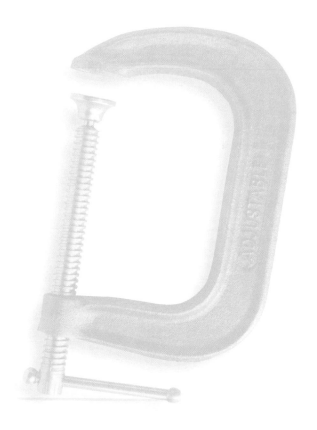

Blurry Photo

This is a blurry image, which will compress differently than other types of images.

Crisp Photo

This is a crisp photographic image, which will compress differently than other types of images.

Illustration

This is an illustration, which will compress differently than other types of images.

You can use the following pages as guides to compressing your own images. If you have a specific image in mind, compare it to this page to see which type of image category it falls under. Turn to those pages and compare the file savings of GIF and JPEG compression methods. This should help you find a ballpark compression setting and save you the time of putting each of your images through all these settings!

blurry photo compression guide

This compression test shows that the JPEG format compressed this image the best, with the highest quality results. This image looks great at a low JPEG setting, and only measures 18.9k. If you needed to save this image as a GIF, for animation or transparency reasons, the best choice would be a 6-bit, adaptive palette, using diffusion, at 37.8k. Even though the examples with no diffusion compress the best, blurry imagery looks bad without diffusion.

jpg max • 32.9k   **jpg high • 25.6k**   **jpg med • 20.8k**   **jpg low • 18.9k**

gif 8-bit • adapt dith • 47.9k   **gif 7-bit • adapt dith • 41.8k**   **gif 6-bit • adapt dith • 37.8k**   **gif 5-bit • adapt dith • 33.5k**

gif 4-bit • adapt dith • 27.5k   **gif 3-bit • adapt dith • 24.4k**   **gif 2-bit • adapt dith • 24.4k**   **gif 1-bit • adapt dith • 19.8k**

gif 8-bit • adapt none • 40.1k   **gif 7-bit • adapt none • 32.15k**   **gif 6-bit • adapt none • 28.2k**   **gif 5-bit • adapt none • 23.8k**

gif 4-bit • adapt none • 19.8k   **gif 3-bit • adapt none • 16.8k**   **gif 2-bit • adapt none • 12.2k**   **gif 1-bit • adapt none • 14.9k**

crisp photo compression guide

As with most photographs, JPEG will compress the best and this image looks fine at a low setting. In this case, the low setting measures 25.4k. If you needed to save this image instead as a GIF, for animation or transparency purposes, it pays to use no dithering. My favorite picks here are the 6-bit GIFs—with dithering its measurement is 38.3k, and without it's 32.3k.

jpg max • 44.6k

jpg high • 34.2k

jpg med • 28.2k

jpg low • 25.4k

gif 8-bit • adapt dith • 49.4k

gif 7-bit • adapt dith • 43.0k

gif 6-bit • adapt dith • 38.3k

gif 5-bit • adapt dith • 35.4k

gif 4-bit • adapt dith • 29.2k   **gif 3-bit • adapt dith • 25.6k**   **gif 2-bit • adapt dith • 20.8k**   **gif 1-bit • adapt dith • 25.4k**

gif 8-bit • adapt none • 45.0k   **gif 7-bit • adapt none • 37.9k**   **gif 6-bit • adapt none • 32.3k**   **gif 5-bit • adapt none • 28.9k**

gif 4-bit • adapt none • 23.1k   **gif 3-bit • adapt none • 19.8k**   **gif 2-bit • adapt none • 14.7k**   **gif 1-bit • adapt none • 18.4k**

illustration compression guide

You wouldn't want to save an illustration as a JPEG, but if you did, the high setting would be the best choice. It measures 23.9k. The medium and low JPEG images show unwanted artifacts. Here's a case where a GIF image saved with no dithering is far superior looking to dithering, plus it is much smaller. My best GIF pick is the 5-bit setting with no compression, measuring 14.3k.

jpg max • 29.9k

jpg high • 23.9k

jpg med • 20.0k

jpg low • 18.3k

gif 8-bit • adapt dith • 35.5k

gif 7-bit • adapt dith • 27.8k

gif 6-bit • adapt dith • 25.1k

gif 5-bit • adapt dith • 17.5k

gif 4-bit • adapt dith • 15.4k

gif 3-bit • adapt dith • 18.0k

gif 2-bit • adapt dith • 19.8k

gif 1-bit • adapt dith • 22.4k

gif 8-bit • adapt none • 21.8k

gif 7-bit • adapt none • 19.0k

gif 6-bit • adapt none • 16.8k

gif 5-bit • adapt none • 14.3k

gif 4-bit • adapt none • 12.7k

gif 3-bit • adapt none • 11.0k

gif 2-bit • adapt none • 10.1k

gif 1-bit • adapt dith • 11.8k

summary

This chapter covered the complex decisions involved in creating compressed images. Understanding the following principles will help you choose the best production methods for producing web-bound images.

- Learn to read the "true" size of your images—don't go by the numbers listed in your desktop folders or directories.

- Anti-aliasing adds to your file's size and isn't always necessary.

- Images with noise or a lot of patterns don't compress well using GIF. If possible, use GIF on images with a lot of flat color, such as cartoons, illustrations, and logos.

- When indexing colors in images before creating GIFs, choose the least amount of colors needed to make the image acceptable in quality. This will dramatically lower the file size.

- Don't assume that you need the highest quality settings when using JPEG compression on photographs or continuous-tone images with soft or blurry edges. Try the lowest amount of JPEG compression to see whether you can achieve acceptable quality.

computer color

Creating color artwork for the web is very different from other color delivery mediums because you're publishing your work to computer screens instead of printed pages. Computer screen-based color is composed of projected light and pixels instead of ink pigments, dot patterns, and screen percentages.

In many ways, working with screen-based color can be more fun than working with printed inks. No waiting for color proofs or working with CMYK values that are much less vibrant than RGB. No high-resolution files. No dot screens to deal with. While working on the computer for computer delivery is a lot easier in some ways, don't be fooled into thinking that what you see on your screen is what other people will see on theirs. Just like its print-based counterpart, computer screen-based color has its own set of nasties and gremlins.

Here's a short list of the things that are different about the web as a publishing medium as it pertains to color:

✎   People view your artwork with monitors that have a wide variety of bit-depth settings.

✎   Various computer monitors have differing color calibration and gamma default settings.

✎   Different operating systems affect the way colors are displayed.

✎   Different web browsers affect the way color is displayed.

Creating color images and screens for the web can be done without understanding the medium's limitations, but the results may not be what you are hoping for. The focus of this chapter is to describe the web and computer color environment, and to clue you in on known pitfalls and solutions that will offer maximum control over how your artwork is ultimately seen.

Cross-Platform Color

RGB versus CMYK

The color of a pixel is made up of three projected colors of light that mix together optically. The projected lights form the colors red, green, and blue. Once mixed together, these three colors create a color space called RGB. Sometimes you'll also hear about CMYK color space, which is formed from cyan, magenta, yellow, and black. CMYK color space on a computer is used to simulate printing inks and is used commonly in print design. Web design is "screen" based, hence RGB color space is always used.

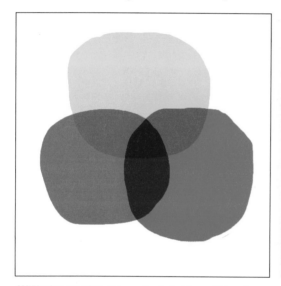

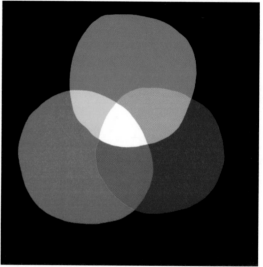

CMYK colors are subtractive, meaning that mixing multiple colors creates black. This color space was created for computer graphics that will be printed on paper.

RGB color is additive, meaning that mixing multiple colors creates white. This color space was created for computer graphics that will be viewed on computer screens.

browser-safe specs

Browser software is your window into the web. You can't see web pages without the browser, so the browser plays a huge role in how your images are displayed, especially when viewed on 256-color systems.

Anyone who has a 256-color (8-bit) video card cannot see images in millions or thousands of colors, even if you prepare images in those bit depths. Because most of your web viewing audience is on minimally configured PCs, it's possible that the majority of your potential audience will be able to view the web in only 256 colors.

In 256-color mode, most popular browsers (Netscape, Mosaic, and Internet Explorer) all share the same palette management process. They work with the system palettes of each respective platform: Mac, Windows, and Win95. This means that any artwork you create will be forced into a variety of different palettes, depending on which operating system it is viewed from.

Mac System Palette

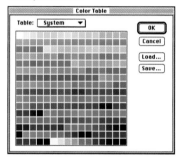

Win95 Palette

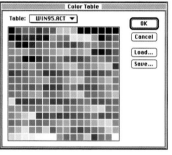

Windows Palette

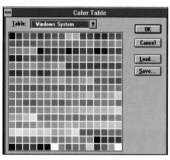

Although these three palettes look entirely different, they share 216 common colors. If you use the shared colors, referred to in this book as "browser-safe" colors, you will eliminate a lot of cross-platform inconsistencies with color artwork published over the web.

Thankfully, there are common colors found within each respective 256 system palette—216 common colors, in fact. Each operating system reserves 40 colors out of the possible 256 for its own use. This means that if you stick to the 216 common colors, they will be universally honored between browsers, operating systems, and computer platforms.

the browser-safe palette

The 216-color palette for the web has only 6 red values, 6 green values, and 6 blue values that range in contrast. Sometimes this palette is referred to as the 6×6×6 palette, or the 6×6×6 cube. This palette is a predetermined palette which, as of yet, can't be changed.

The RGB values found within the 216-color palette have some predictable similarities: the numbers are all formed from variations of 00, 51, 102, 153, 204, and 255.

The hexadecimal values found within the 216-color palette also have predictable similarities: they are all formed from variations of 00, 33, 66, 99, CC, and FF.

These colors were picked by math, not aesthetic considerations. Knowing the pattern of the numeric values is useful because you can easily check your code or image documents to see whether they contain these values.

Notice how the colors in the chart to the right have no sense of organization? They are organized by math, not beauty.

On the pages that follow you will find the same 216 colors, organized in a more useful way: by color (hue) and value (lights–medium tones–darks).

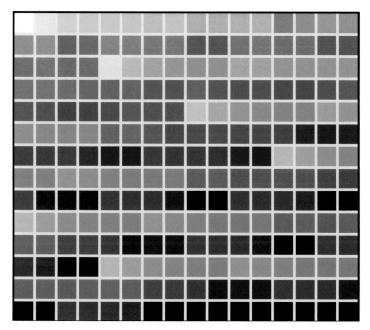

Here is a version of the browser-safe color palette, straight out of the computer; it is organized mathematically, not aesthetically.

note

Do Browser-Safe Colors Really Matter?

You may think that all this hubbub over browser-safe colors need not apply to you. If you think your site will be viewed only from millions-of-color monitors (24-bit), you might be right. It's always important to decide who your audience is before you design a site and create artwork that is appropriate for your viewers.

My recommendation is, if you are going to pick colors for backgrounds, type, text, links, and illustrations, why not choose cross-platform compatible colors? There may come a day years from now when everyone has video cards that support more than 256 colors, but the majority of systems today do not.

Browser-Safe Colors Organized by Hue

330000 R=051 G=000 B=000	**660000** R=102 G=000 B=000	**990000** R=153 G=000 B=000	**CC0000** R=204 G=000 B=000	**FF0000** R=255 G=000 B=000	**663333** R=102 G=051 B=051	**993333** R=153 G=051 B=051	**CC3333** R=204 G=051 B=051
CC0033 R=204 G=000 B=051	**FF3366** R=255 G=051 B=102	**990033** R=153 G=000 B=051	**CC3366** R=204 G=051 B=102	**FF6699** R=255 G=102 B=153	**FF0066** R=255 G=000 B=102	**660033** R=102 G=000 B=051	**CC0066** R=204 G=000 B=102
CC0099 R=204 G=000 B=153	**FF33CC** R=255 G=51 B=204	**FF00CC** R=255 G=000 B=204	**330033** R=051 G=000 B=051	**660066** R=102 G=000 B=102	**990099** R=153 G=000 B=153	**CC00CC** R=204 G=000 B=204	**FF00FF** R=255 G=000 B=255
FF99FF R=255 G=153 B=255	**FFCCFF** R=255 G=204 B=255	**CC00FF** R=204 G=000 B=255	**9900CC** R=153 G=000 B=204	**CC33FF** R=204 G=051 B=255	**660099** R=102 G=000 B=153	**9933CC** R=153 G=051 B=204	**CC66FF** R=204 G=102 B=255
330099 R=051 G=000 B=153	**6633CC** R=102 G=051 B=204	**9966FF** R=153 G=102 B=255	**3300CC** R=051 G=000 B=204	**6633FF** R=102 G=051 B=255	**3300FF** R=051 G=000 B=255	**000000** R=000 G=000 B=000	**000033** R=000 G=000 B=051
666699 R=102 G=102 B=153	**6666CC** R=102 G=102 B=204	**6666FF** R=102 G=102 B=255	**9999CC** R=153 G=153 B=204	**9999FF** R=153 G=153 B=255	**CCCCFF** R=204 G=204 B=255	**0033FF** R=000 G=051 B=255	**0033CC** R=000 G=051 B=204
3399FF R=051 G=153 B=255	**6699CC** R=102 G=153 B=204	**99CCFF** R=153 G=204 B=255	**0099FF** R=000 G=153 B=255	**006699** R=000 G=102 B=153	**3399CC** R=051 G=153 B=204	**66CCFF** R=102 G=204 B=255	**0099CC** R=000 G=153 B=204
00CCCC R=000 G=204 B=204	**33CCCC** R=051 G=204 B=204	**66CCCC** R=102 G=204 B=204	**99CCCC** R=153 G=204 B=204	**00FFFF** R=000 G=255 B=255	**33FFFF** R=051 G=255 B=255	**66FFFF** R=102 G=255 B=255	**99FFFF** R=153 G=255 B=255
006633 R=000 G=102 B=051	**339966** R=051 G=153 B=102	**00CC66** R=000 G=204 B=102	**66CC99** R=102 G=204 B=153	**33FF99** R=051 G=255 B=153	**99FFCC** R=153 G=255 B=204	**00FF66** R=000 G=255 B=102	**009933** R=000 G=153 B=051
009900 R=000 G=153 B=000	**339933** R=051 G=153 B=051	**669966** R=102 G=153 B=102	**00CC00** R=000 G=204 B=000	**33CC33** R=051 G=204 B=051	**66CC66** R=102 G=204 B=102	**99CC99** R=153 G=204 B=153	**00FF00** R=000 G=255 B=000
66CC33 R=102 G=204 B=051	**99FF66** R=153 G=255 B=102	**66FF00** R=102 G=255 B=000	**336600** R=051 G=102 B=000	**669933** R=102 G=153 B=051	**66CC00** R=102 G=204 B=000	**99CC66** R=153 G=204 B=102	**99FF33** R=153 G=255 B=051
333300 R=051 G=051 B=000	**666600** R=102 G=102 B=000	**666633** R=102 G=102 B=051	**999900** R=153 G=153 B=000	**999933** R=153 G=153 B=051	**999966** R=153 G=153 B=102	**CCCC00** R=204 G=204 B=000	**CCCC33** R=204 G=204 B=051
CC9900 R=204 G=153 B=000	**FFCC33** R=255 G=204 B=051	**996600** R=153 G=102 B=000	**CC9933** R=204 G=153 B=051	**FFCC66** R=255 G=204 B=102	**FF9900** R=255 G=153 B=000	**663300** R=102 G=051 B=000	**996633** R=153 G=102 B=051
CC3300 R=204 G=051 B=000	**FF6633** R=255 G=102 B=051	**FF3300** R=255 G=051 B=000	**333333** R=051 G=051 B=051	**666666** R=102 G=102 B=102	**999999** R=153 G=153 B=153	**CCCCCC** R=204 G=204 B=204	**FFFFFF** R=255 G=255 B=255

92

FF3333 R=255 G=051 B=051	**996666** R=153 G=102 B=102	**CC6666** R=204 G=102 B=102	**FF6666** R=255 G=102 B=102	**CC9999** R=204 G=153 B=153	**FF9999** R=255 G=153 B=153	**FFCCCC** R=255 G=204 B=204	**FF0033** R=255 G=000 B=051
993366 R=153 G=051 B=102	**FF3399** R=255 G=051 B=153	**CC6699** R=204 G=102 B=153	**FF99CC** R=255 G=153 B=204	**FF0099** R=255 G=000 B=153	**990066** R=153 G=000 B=102	**CC3399** R=204 G=051 B=153	**FF66CC** R=255 G=102 B=204
663366 R=102 G=051 B=102	**993399** R=153 G=051 B=153	**CC33CC** R=204 G=051 B=204	**FF33FF** R=255 G=051 B=255	**996699** R=153 G=102 B=153	**CC66CC** R=204 G=102 B=204	**FF66FF** R=255 G=102 B=255	**CC99CC** R=204 G=153 B=204
9900FF R=153 G=000 B=255	**330066** R=051 G=000 B=102	**6600CC** R=102 G=000 B=204	**663399** R=102 G=051 B=153	**9933FF** R=153 G=051 B=255	**9966CC** R=153 G=102 B=204	**CC99FF** R=204 G=153 B=255	**6600FF** R=102 G=000 B=255
000066 R=000 G=000 B=102	**000099** R=000 G=000 B=153	**0000CC** R=000 G=000 B=204	**0000FF** R=000 G=000 B=255	**333366** R=051 G=051 B=102	**333399** R=051 G=051 B=153	**3333CC** R=051 G=051 B=204	**3333FF** R=051 G=051 B=255
3366FF R=051 G=102 B=255	**003399** R=000 G=051 B=153	**3366CC** R=051 G=102 B=204	**6699FF** R=102 G=153 B=255	**0066FF** R=000 G=051 B=255	**003366** R=000 G=051 B=102	**0066CC** R=000 G=102 B=204	**336699** R=051 G=102 B=153
33CCFF R=051 G=204 B=255	**00CCFF** R=000 G=204 B=255	**003333** R=000 G=051 B=051	**006666** R=000 G=102 B=102	**336666** R=051 G=102 B=102	**009999** R=000 G=153 B=153	**339999** R=051 G=153 B=153	**669999** R=102 G=153 B=153
CCFFFF R=204 G=255 B=255	**00FFCC** R=000 G=255 B=204	**00CC99** R=000 G=204 B=153	**33FFCC** R=051 G=255 B=204	**009966** R=000 G=153 B=102	**33CC99** R=051 G=204 B=153	**66FFCC** R=102 G=255 B=204	**00FF99** R=000 G=255 B=153
33CC66 R=051 G=204 B=102	**66FF99** R=102 G=255 B=153	**00CC33** R=000 G=204 B=051	**33FF66** R=051 G=255 B=102	**00FF33** R=000 G=255 B=051	**003300** R=000 G=051 B=000	**006600** R=000 G=102 B=000	**336633** R=051 G=102 B=051
33FF33 R=051 G=255 B=051	**66FF66** R=102 G=255 B=102	**99FF99** R=153 G=255 B=153	**CCFFCC** R=204 G=255 B=204	**33FF00** R=051 G=255 B=000	**33CC00** R=051 G=204 B=000	**66FF33** R=102 G=255 B=051	**339900** R=051 G=153 B=000
CCFF99 R=204 G=255 B=153	**99FF00** R=153 G=255 B=000	**669900** R=102 G=153 B=000	**99CC33** R=153 G=204 B=051	**CCFF66** R=204 G=255 B=102	**99CC00** R=153 G=204 B=000	**CCFF33** R=204 G=255 B=051	**CCFF00** R=204 G=255 B=000
CCCC66 R=204 G=204 B=102	**CCCC99** R=204 G=204 B=153	**FFFF00** R=255 G=255 B=000	**FFFF33** R=255 G=255 B=051	**FFFF66** R=255 G=255 B=102	**FFFF99** R=255 G=255 B=153	**FFFFCC** R=255 G=255 B=204	**FFCC00** R=255 G=204 B=000
CC6600 R=204 G=102 B=000	**CC9966** R=204 G=153 B=102	**FF9933** R=255 G=153 B=051	**FFCC99** R=255 G=204 B=153	**FF6600** R=255 G=102 B=000	**993300** R=153 G=051 B=000	**CC6633** R=204 G=102 B=051	**FF9966** R=255 G=153 B=102

preparing web graphics

Browser-Safe Colors Organized by Value

FFFFFF R=255 G=255 B=255	**FFFFCC** R=255 G=255 B=204	**FFFF99** R=255 G=255 B=153	**CCFFFF** R=204 G=255 B=255	**FFFF66** R=255 G=255 B=102	**CCFFCC** R=204 G=255 B=204	**FFFF33** R=255 G=255 B=051	**CCFF99** R=204 G=255 B=153
99FF99 R=153 G=255 B=153	**CCFF00** R=204 G=255 B=000	**CCCCFF** R=204 G=204 B=255	**66FFFF** R=102 G=255 B=255	**FFCC66** R=255 G=204 B=102	**99FF66** R=153 G=255 B=102	**CCCCCC** R=204 G=204 B=204	**66FFCC** R=102 G=255 B=204
33FFFF R=051 G=255 B=255	**CCCC66** R=204 G=204 B=102	**66FF66** R=102 G=255 B=102	**FF99CC** R=255 G=153 B=204	**99CCCC** R=153 G=204 B=204	**33FFCC** R=051 G=255 B=204	**CCCC33** R=204 G=204 B=051	**66FF33** R=102 G=255 B=051
FF9966 R=255 G=153 B=102	**99CC66** R=153 G=204 B=102	**33FF66** R=051 G=255 B=102	**CC99CC** R=204 G=153 B=204	**66CCCC** R=102 G=204 B=204	**00FFCC** R=000 G=255 B=204	**FF9933** R=255 G=153 B=051	**99CC33** R=153 G=204 B=051
9999FF R=153 G=153 B=255	**33CCFF** R=051 G=204 B=255	**CC9966** R=204 G=153 B=102	**66CC66** R=102 G=204 B=102	**00FF66** R=000 G=255 B=102	**FF66CC** R=255 G=102 B=204	**9999CC** R=153 G=153 B=204	**33CCCC** R=051 G=204 B=204
00FF00 R=000 G=255 B=000	**CC66FF** R=204 G=102 B=255	**6699FF** R=102 G=153 B=255	**00CCFF** R=000 G=204 B=255	**FF6666** R=255 G=102 B=102	**999966** R=153 G=153 B=102	**33CC66** R=051 G=204 B=102	**CC66CC** R=204 G=102 B=204
FF6600 R=255 G=102 B=000	**999900** R=153 G=153 B=000	**33CC00** R=051 G=204 B=000	**FF33FF** R=255 G=051 B=255	**9966FF** R=153 G=102 B=255	**3399FF** R=051 G=153 B=255	**CC6666** R=204 G=102 B=102	**669966** R=102 G=153 B=102
996699 R=153 G=102 B=153	**339999** R=051 G=153 B=153	**CC6600** R=204 G=102 B=000	**669900** R=102 G=153 B=000	**00CC00** R=000 G=204 B=000	**CC33FF** R=204 G=051 B=255	**6666FF** R=102 G=102 B=255	**0099FF** R=000 G=153 B=255
339933 R=051 G=153 B=051	**CC3399** R=204 G=051 B=153	**666699** R=102 G=102 B=153	**009999** R=000 G=153 B=153	**FF3300** R=255 G=051 B=000	**996600** R=153 G=102 B=000	**339900** R=051 G=153 B=000	**FF00FF** R=255 G=000 B=255
CC3333 R=204 G=051 B=051	**666633** R=102 G=102 B=051	**009933** R=000 G=153 B=051	**FF0099** R=255 G=000 B=153	**993399** R=153 G=051 B=153	**336699** R=051 G=102 B=153	**CC3300** R=204 G=051 B=000	**666600** R=102 G=102 B=000
6633CC R=102 G=051 B=204	**0066CC** R=000 G=102 B=204	**FF0033** R=255 G=000 B=051	**993333** R=153 G=051 B=051	**336633** R=051 G=102 B=051	**CC0099** R=204 G=000 B=153	**663399** R=102 G=051 B=153	**006699** R=000 G=102 B=153
9900CC R=153 G=000 B=204	**3333CC** R=051 G=051 B=204	**CC0033** R=204 G=000 B=051	**663333** R=102 G=051 B=051	**006633** R=000 G=102 B=051	**990099** R=153 G=000 B=153	**333399** R=051 G=051 B=153	**CC0000** R=204 G=000 B=000
990033 R=153 G=000 B=051	**333333** R=051 G=051 B=051	**660099** R=102 G=000 B=153	**003399** R=000 G=051 B=153	**990000** R=153 G=000 B=000	**333300** R=051 G=051 B=000	**3300FF** R=051 G=000 B=255	**660066** R=102 G=000 B=102
330066 R=051 G=000 B=102	**0000CC** R=000 G=000 B=204	**330033** R=051 G=000 B=051	**000099** R=000 G=000 B=153	**330000** R=051 G=000 B=000	**000066** R=000 G=000 B=102	**000033** R=000 G=000 B=051	**000000** R=000 G=000 B=000

FFFF00 R=255 G=255 B=000	**FFCCFF** R=255 G=204 B=255	**99FFFF** R=153 G=255 B=255	**CCFF00** R=204 G=255 B=102	**FFCCCC** R=255 G=204 B=204	**99FFCC** R=153 G=255 B=204	**CCFF33** R=204 G=255 B=051	**FFCC99** R=255 G=204 B=153
FFCC33 R=255 G=204 B=051	**99FF33** R=153 G=255 B=051	**CCCC99** R=204 G=204 B=153	**66FF99** R=102 G=255 B=153	**FFCC00** R=255 G=204 B=000	**99FF00** R=153 G=255 B=000	**FF99FF** R=255 G=153 B=255	**99CCFF** R=153 G=204 B=255
FF9999 R=255 G=153 B=153	**99CC99** R=153 G=204 B=153	**33FF99** R=051 G=255 B=153	**CCCC00** R=204 G=204 B=000	**66FF00** R=102 G=255 B=000	**CC99FF** R=204 G=153 B=255	**66CCFF** R=102 G=204 B=255	**00FFFF** R=000 G=255 B=255
33FF33 R=051 G=255 B=051	**CC9999** R=204 G=153 B=153	**66CC99** R=102 G=204 B=153	**00FF99** R=000 G=255 B=153	**FF9900** R=255 G=153 B=000	**99CC00** R=153 G=204 B=000	**33FF00** R=051 G=255 B=000	**FF66FF** R=255 G=102 B=255
CC9933 R=204 G=153 B=051	**66CC33** R=102 G=204 B=051	**00FF33** R=000 G=255 B=051	**FF6699** R=255 G=102 B=153	**999999** R=153 G=153 B=153	**33CC99** R=051 G=204 B=153	**CC9900** R=204 G=153 B=000	**66CC00** R=102 G=204 B=000
6699CC R=102 G=153 B=204	**00CCCC** R=000 G=204 B=204	**FF6633** R=255 G=102 B=051	**999933** R=153 G=153 B=051	**33CC33** R=051 G=204 B=051	**CC6699** R=204 G=102 B=153	**669999** R=102 G=153 B=153	**00CC99** R=000 G=204 B=153
00CC66 R=000 G=204 B=102	**FF33CC** R=255 G=051 B=204	**9966CC** R=153 G=102 B=204	**3399CC** R=051 G=153 B=204	**CC6633** R=204 G=102 B=051	**669933** R=102 G=153 B=051	**00CC33** R=000 G=204 B=051	**FF3399** R=255 G=051 B=153
FF3366 R=255 G=051 B=102	**996666** R=153 G=102 B=102	**339966** R=051 G=153 B=102	**CC33CC** R=204 G=051 B=204	**6666CC** R=102 G=102 B=204	**0099CC** R=000 G=153 B=204	**FF3333** R=255 G=051 B=051	**996633** R=153 G=102 B=051
9933FF R=153 G=051 B=255	**3366FF** R=051 G=102 B=255	**CC3366** R=204 G=051 B=102	**666666** R=102 G=102 B=102	**009966** R=000 G=153 B=102	**FF00CC** R=255 G=000 B=204	**9933CC** R=153 G=051 B=204	**3366CC** R=051 G=102 B=204
009900 R=000 G=153 B=000	**CC00FF** R=204 G=000 B=255	**6633FF** R=102 G=051 B=255	**0066FF** R=000 G=102 B=255	**FF0066** R=255 G=000 B=102	**993366** R=153 G=051 B=102	**336666** R=051 G=102 B=102	**CC00CC** R=204 G=000 B=204
FF0000 R=255 G=000 B=000	**993300** R=153 G=051 B=000	**336600** R=051 G=102 B=000	**9900FF** R=153 G=000 B=255	**3333FF** R=051 G=051 B=255	**CC0066** R=204 G=000 B=102	**663366** R=102 G=051 B=102	**006666** R=000 G=102 B=102
663300 R=102 G=051 B=000	**006600** R=000 G=102 B=000	**6600FF** R=102 G=000 B=255	**0033FF** R=000 G=051 B=255	**990066** R=153 G=000 B=102	**333366** R=051 G=051 B=102	**6600CC** R=102 G=000 B=204	**0033CC** R=000 G=051 B=204
003366 R=000 G=051 B=102	**3300CC** R=051 G=000 B=204	**660033** R=102 G=000 B=051	**003333** R=000 G=000 B=051	**330099** R=051 G=000 B=153	**660000** R=102 G=000 B=000	**003300** R=000 G=051 B=000	**0000FF** R=000 G=000 B=255

hexadecimal-based color

Web page color schemes are generally chosen by using hexadecimal values instead of embedded artwork. If you choose a one-color background on your millions-of-color monitor and the end user views the image on a 256-color monitor, the browser will convert it to one of the 216 colors anyway. It will shift the colors you've chosen to its own fixed palette.

Hexadecimal code is used instead of RGB values within HTML. Here's a site that used the following hexadecimal code:

`<BODY BGCOLOR="#090301" TEXT="#436E58" LINK="#CF7B42" ="#323172" ALINK="#ffffff">`

You should be able to tell, just by looking, that these colors are not browser safe! Remember, browser-safe hex combinations are always formed from variations of 00, 33, 66, 99, CC, and FF.

Mac • 8-bit display

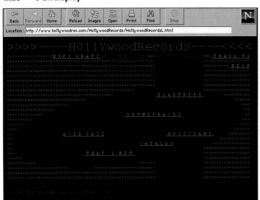

PC • 8-bit display

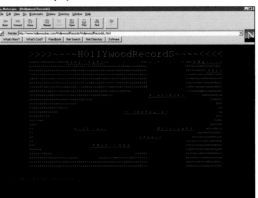

This comparison demonstrates the kind of color shifting that occurs with hexadecimal-based artwork, on 8-bit systems, if the colors used are not browser safe.

illustration-based artwork

Illustration-based artwork, such as logos, cartoons, or drawings, respond differently inside web browsers when viewed in 256 colors. Because the browser can display only colors of each respective operating system's native palette, it forces artwork you created in other palettes into its own. Unlike hexadecimal color, which shifts colors into its own fixed palette, color image files dither instead. Dithering is a process where the computer attempts to display a color outside its color range by placing different colored dots next to each other. This is calculated mathematically and often looks extremely unappealing.

If you use the browser-safe, 216-color palette when creating illustration-based artwork, you will avoid unexpected and unwanted dithering. Later in this chapter, you will find a lot of tips and techniques that will help you learn to draw, paint, and type using browser-safe colors.

Here's a close-up of the dithering present in the nonbrowser-safe version of this illustration, when viewed on 8-bit systems.

On a millions-of-color display, you might not notice any differences between these two different illustrations of the Lynda's Homegurrrl Page logo.

On an 8-bit display, look at what happens to the top version. It is filled with unwanted dots, caused by dithering. Why? The colors in the bottom logo are browser safe, and the colors in the top are not.

The close-up of the version created with browser-safe colors will not dither, regardless of which bit depth the end viewer's system supports.

photograph-based artwork

Photographs are the one type of artwork that really does not benefit from using browser-safe colors. The reason is that the browsers convert photographs to each respective operating system's native color palette, but do a great job of it—unlike the terrible job they do with hexadecimal-based artwork and illustration-based artwork.

The images in the top row of this study were all viewed from a browser in 24-bit. Which ones on the top row have the highest quality? The JPEG, which is a 24-bit file, and the adaptive file, which is an 8-bit file based on the colors within the image, not an outside palette as in the case of the images saved with the browser-safe palette. The images on the bottom row show how these photographs look within a browser viewed from a millions+ color system (24-bit). The top row images all look worse than when viewed in the 24-bit browser, but are there any significant quality benefits from having saved them with different methods? I think not. The results of this study? It is not necessary to convert photographic-based images to the browser-safe palette or even to an 8-bit palette. The browser does its dithering dirty work, regardless of how you prepare the image. It's best to leave the image in an adaptive palette or 24-bit file format so that the photographs will have the added advantage of looking better in 24-bit browser environments. JPEGs will always produce the smallest file size for photographs and have the added advantage of being a 24-bit file format, unlike GIF, which cannot save images at higher bit depths than 8-bit (256 colors).

Viewed in 24-bit

adaptive 8-bit file • 35k

browser-safe palette • 50k

JPEG (low quality) • 11k

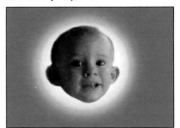

Viewed in 8-bit

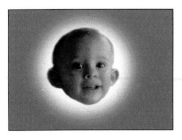

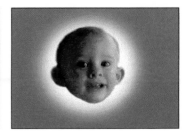

working browser safe

Now that you've seen the damage that can be wreaked by working or not working with browser-safe color, how do you create artwork that uses cross-platform compatible color? The previous sections are summarized by the following points:

✎ Hexadecimal color should contain the browser-safe values 00, 33, 66,99, CC, and FF so that it doesn't shift unexpectedly.

✎ Illustration-based artwork should use the browser-safe values 00, 51, 102, 153, 204, and 255 so it doesn't dither unexpectedly.

✎ Photographs look best with an 8-bit adaptive palette or in 24-bit (which doesn't use palettes at all, but can choose from any of 16.7 million colors). By forcing photographs into the 216 palette, images are reduced to the lowest common denominator so that end users with better color systems are forced to see the same poor quality that those with 256 video cards see.

The following sections go into depth about how to create colored artwork, web pages, and photographs that will look best under most color conditions that end users will encounter when viewing your content.

browser safe with hex

Working with color on the web is not nearly as intuitive as specifying color in Photoshop and other imaging programs. If you want to use colors—as in colored text, colored links, colored backgrounds, and colored borders—describing them by their hexadecimal values is the only way HTML lets you do it. You can also add colored backgrounds by loading an image into the background of your page (see Chapter 7, "Background Tiles"), but if you want solid colors, using hexadecimal code is the most efficient way because the colors will download faster.

Hexadecimal is based on base 16 mathematics. Here's a little table that shows how hexadecimal math works.

#	0	1	2	3	4	5	6	7	8	9	10	11	12	13	14	15
HEX	0	1	2	3	4	5	6	7	8	9	A	B	C	D	E	F

In this chart the numbers on the top are base 10 and the numbers on the bottom are base 16, aka hexadecimal.

Hexadecimal Chart

Hexadecimal numbers in web design are used to convert RGB values so that HTML can understand which colors you've chosen. Here is a helpful chart for dealing with RGB number conversions (0–255) to hex. The browser-safe colors are highlighted.

00=00	01=01	02=02	03=03	04=04	05=05	06=06	07=07
08=08	09=09	10=0A	11=0B	12=0C	13=0D	14=0E	15=0F
16=10	17=11	18=12	19=13	20=14	21=15	22=16	23=17
24=18	25=19	26=1A	27=1B	28=1C	29=1D	30=1E	31=1F
32=20	33=21	34=22	35=23	36=24	37=25	38=26	39=27
40=28	41=29	42=2A	43=2B	44=2C	45=2D	46=2E	47=2F
48=30	49=31	50=32	**51=33**	52=34	53=35	54=36	55=37
56=38	57=39	58=3A	59=3B	60=3C	61=3D	62=3E	63=3F
64=40	65=41	66=42	67=43	68=44	69=45	70=46	71=47
72=48	73=49	74=4A	75=4B	76=4C	77=4D	78=4E	79=4F
80=50	81=51	82=52	83=53	84=54	85=55	86=56	87=57
88=58	89=59	90=5A	91=5B	92=5C	93=5D	94=5E	95=5F
96=60	97=61	98=62	99=63	100=64	101=65	**102=66**	103=67
104=68	105=69	106=6A	107=6B	108=6C	109=6D	110=6E	111=6F
112=70	113=71	114=72	115=73	116=74	117=75	118=76	119=77
120=78	121=79	122=7A	123=7B	124=7C	125=7D	126=7E	127=7F
128=80	129=81	130=82	131=83	132=84	133=85	134=86	135=87
136=88	137=89	138=8A	139=8B	140=8C	141=8D	142=8E	143=8F
144=90	145=91	146=92	147=93	148=94	149=95	150=96	151=97
152=98	**153=99**	154=9A	155=9B	156=9C	157=9D	158=9E	159=9F
160=A0	161=A1	162=A2	163=A3	164=A4	165=A5	166=A6	167=A7
168=A8	168=A9	170=AA	171=AB	172=AC	173=AD	17=AE	175=AF
176=B0	177=B1	178=B2	179=B3	180=B4	181=B5	182=B6	183=B7
184=B8	185=B9	186=BA	187=BB	188=BC	189=BD	190=BE	191=BF
192=C0	193=C1	194=C2	195=C3	196=C4	197=C5	198=C6	199=C7
200=C8	201=C9	202=CA	203=CB	**204=CC**	205=CD	206=CE	207=CF
208=D0	209=D1	210=D2	211=D3	212=D4	213=D5	214=D6	215=D7
216=D8	217=D9	218=DA	219=DB	220=DC	221=DD	222=DE	223=DF
224=E0	225=E1	226=E2	227=E3	228=E4	229=E5	230=E6	231=E7
232=E8	233=E9	234=EA	235=EB	236=EC	237=ED	238=EE	239=EF
240=F0	241=F1	242=F2	243=F3	244=F4	245=F5	246=F6	247=F7
248=F8	249=F9	250=FA	251=FB	252=FC	253=FD	254=FE	**255=FF**

hexadecimal resources

Many web resources exist for converting RGB values to hex numbers. There are two different options: hex charts, which typically show color swatches and their hex values, and hex converters. Hex converters allow a user to type RGB numbers and then offer the hexadecimal conversion in return. Both options are covered in the following sections.

Web Hex Converters

There are a number of sites on the web that let you plug RGB values into them and then generate hex code for your values on-the-fly. This can be convenient when you're working and want a quick visualization of what a certain color scheme will look like. Some sites even go so far as to accept RGB input and then automatically output hex and HTML.

✎ **Inquisitor Mediarama's RGB-HEX Converter**
   ✍ http://www.echonyc.com/~xixax/Mediarama/hex.html

✎ **Test your hex color choices on-the-fly**
   ✍ http://www.hidaho.com/c3/

✎ **Click on any color, and hex numbers will appear**
   ✍ http://www.schnoggo.com/rgb2hex.html

✎ **Browser-Safe Color JavaScript Hex Converter**
   ✍ http://www.hanson-dodge.com/colors/index.html

Hex Calculators

There are also hexadecimal calculators that take the RGB values you enter and convert the math automatically. Once you have converted your RGB numbers, you are ready to use the resulting hex in your HTML code.

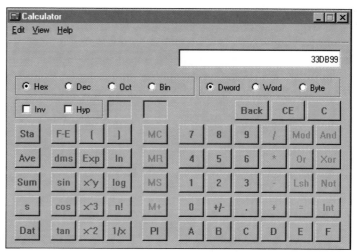

PCs ship with a hex calculator, which usually is found in the Accessories group. Open the Calculator and then under View, select Scientific. This changes the standard calculator to a scientific calculator. Then, simply select the Hex option to start converting your RGB values.

Mac users can download a great hex calculator written by Joseph Cicinelli, called Calculator II, from ftp://ftp.amug.org/pub/mirrors/info-mac/sci/calc/calculator-ii-15.hqx.

color-related HTML tags

Now for the fun (not) part. How does this all this come together on a web page? Web pages are written in a low-level programming language called HTML (**H**yper**T**ext **M**arkup **L**anguage). You can write HTML code in a standard text editor, dedicated HTML editor, or WYSIWYG (**W**hat**Y**ou**S**ee**I**s**W**hat**Y**ou**G**et) HTML editor. Some WYSIWYG editors allow you to edit HTML source code directly, and some do not. Because some of the color tags discussed in this chapter may not be supported by WYSIWYG editors, you may have to edit your files later to add the foreign HTML tags. You can always begin a page in a WYSIWYG editor and then edit the source code later in a text editor in order to add additional tags.

To describe the color R:255 G:00 B:51, the hexadecimal code would be FF0033. Here's the most minimal sample code for an HTML page that has the following color scheme. More detailed information about how to set up these color tags follow later in this chapter.

```
<HTML>
<BODY BGCOLOR="003333" TEXT="33CCCC" LINK="336699" VLINK="006666" ALINK="00CC99"
</BODY>
</HTML>
```

color-related attributes

BGCOLOR	Color of the background of the web page
TEXT	Color of the text
LINK	Color of the link
VLINK	Color of the link after it has been visited
ALINK	Color of the active link while the mouse is depressed on a link

Possible attributes that relate to color within the <BODY> tag.

The results of the hexadecimal HTML code to create background, text, link, visited link, and active link colors.

bgcolor	text	link	vlink	alink
003333	33CCCC	336699	006666	00CC99
R·0	R·51	R·51	R·0	R·0
G·51	G·204	G·102	G·102	G·204
B·51	B·204	B·153	B·102	B·153

These swatches demonstrate the RGB-to-hex conversion process.

Adding Color to a Web Page Using HTML

To add variety within HTML, you must include special tags called attributes. Attributes modify the existing material—applying italic or bold to text, for example. When used in HTML, attributes are nested within their parent tags. So to add color to the body text, you would place the attribute within the <BODY> tag. To add color to the page in our example, you would add the following HTML code:

```
<HTML>
<HEAD>
<TITLE>Adding Color to My Page</TITLE>
</HEAD>
<BODY BGCOLOR="660099"
TEXT="CCCCFF">
<H1>This page is where I will play with
color using all the nifty color tags I
can learn.
</H1>
</BODY>
```

BGCOLOR and **TEXT** are attributes that are nested inside the **<BODY>** tag. The **BGCOLOR** attribute instructs the background of the HTML page to be colored. The **TEXT** attribute instructs the text to be colored. The content of these tags can contain hexadecimal values that represent RGB colors.

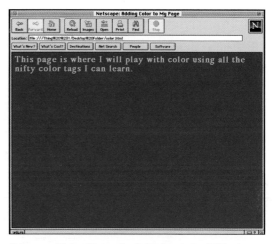

Color was added to this page by placing hexadecimal RGB values inside the BGCOLOR and TEXT attributes within the <BODY> tag.

Using Color Names Instead of Hex

You don't have to use hexadecimal numbers inside the color attribute tags; you can use words, too. Here's a list of color names that will work in Netscape.

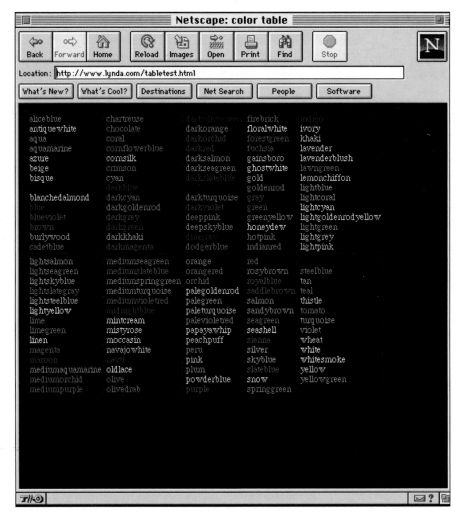

Using any of the names inside the color attribute tags will generate colored text in Netscape.

HTML for Color Names

```
<HTML>
<HEAD>
<TITLE>Adding Color to My Page</TITLE>
</HEAD>
```
❶
```
<BODY BGCOLOR="lightgreen"
TEXT="darkgreen">
<H1>This page is where I will play with
color using all the nifty color tags I
can learn.
</H1>
</BODY>
</HTML>
```

❶ You don't have to use hexadecimal numbers to define color—certain color names work as well. Here's an example of using **"lightgreen"** and **"darkgreen"** as color names within the **<BODY>** tag.

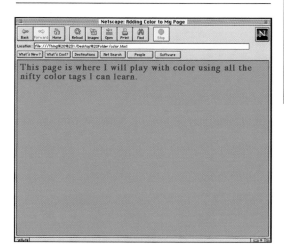

Here's an example of using color names instead of hexadecimal values to define color.

Color Names Are Rarely Browser Safe

Color names work in Netscape and Internet Explorer, but the majority are not browser-safe. This means that color names in your HTML will fall prey to the same problems as using any of the colors that are not browser safe.

cross-platform color names

Black	000000	
White	FFFFFF	
Cyan/Aqua/Blue	0000FF	
Fushia/Magenta	FF00FF	
Red	FF0000	
Lime	00FF00	
Yellow	FFFF00	

This chart records only the color names that are browser safe. Notice a few names are actually the same hexadecimal. They are simply different ways to name the very same color.

preparing web graphics

Coloring Individual Lines of Text

You can also assign specific colors to individual lines of text with the <FONT> tag. Here's some sample code.

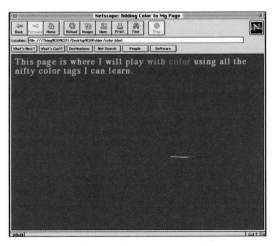

Here's an example of using the <FONT> tag to insert color attributes so that individual words or letters can be colored.

```
<HTML>
<HEAD>
<TITLE>Adding Color to My Page</TITLE>
</HEAD>
<BODY BGCOLOR="660099"
TEXT="CCCCFF">
<H1>This page is where I
<FONT COLOR="99FFFF">will </FONT>
<FONT COLOR="CCFF99">play </FONT>
<FONT COLOR="CC99CC">with </FONT>
<FONT COLOR="CC0000">color </FONT>
using all the nifty color tags I
can learn.
</H1>
</BODY>
</HTML>
```

1 The **<FONT>** tag can contain a color attribute, which can be specified by using color names or hex numbers. It must be closed with a **</FONT>** tag each time you want the specific colored text attribute to end.

Coloring Links

Link color can affect the border color around linked images or the color of linked text. Here's an example of how to set this up in an HTML document.

```
<HTML>
<HEAD>
<TITLE>Adding Color to My Page</TITLE>
</HEAD>
<BODY BGCOLOR="660099"
TEXT="CCCCFF"
```
❶ `LINK="CCFF00">`
```
<H1>Here's an example of a <AHREF="http:
//www.stinkabod.com">text-based  hyper-
link</A>.
<P>
Here's an example of a linked graphic
with a fat, colored border: </H1>
<P>
<A HREF="http://www.stinkabod.com">
```
❷ `<IMG SRC="fourlynda.gif" BORDER=10></A>`
```
</BODY>
</HTML>
```

❶ The **LINK** attribute within the **<BODY>** tag establishes the color for the linked text or graphic. The **<A HREF> </A>** tag produces linked text.

---

❷ The **<IMG SRC>** tag inserts an image, and the **BORDER** attribute enables you to set a width for the border, measured in pixels. Note: If you don't want a border, you can set this to **BORDER=0**.

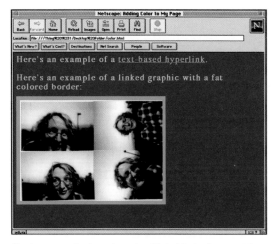

Here's an example of creating colored links. The border around the graphic was made wider with the BORDER attribute.

Inserting a Background Image

If you would like to use an image of a color in the background of your web page, instead of a hex color, this is how you would structure the HTML.

```
<HTML>
<HEAD>
<TITLE>Adding Color to My Page</TITLE>
</HEAD>
<BODY
❶ BACKGROUND="tile.gif"
TEXT="CCCCFF" LINK="CCFF00">
<CENTER>
<A HREF="http://www.stinkabod.com"><IMG
SRC="fourlynda.gif" BORDER=10></A>
<CENTER>
</BODY>
</HTML>
```

❶ The **BACKGROUND** attribute within the **<BODY>** tag enables you to insert an image into the background of the web page. This image can be any kind of image (**.jpg or .gif**), and can be a solid color, a hybrid color, a seamless tile image, or a repeating tile image.

Here's an example of inserting a background image. You can insert a solid color image, a hybrid color image, a seamless tile image, or a repeating tile image. It's the same code, just a different graphic file!

Adding Color to Tables

The BGCOLOR attribute works in table cells as well as the body of the HTML document. Here's some sample code that demonstrates this technique.

```
<HTML>
<HEAD>
<TITLE>Adding Color to My Page</TITLE>
</HEAD>
<BODY BGCOLOR="660099"
TEXT="CCCCFF">
<CENTER>
<TABLE BORDER>
<TR><TH BGCOLOR="003366" HEIGHT=200
WIDTH=200>Hello</TH>
<TH BGCOLOR="990033" HEIGHT=200
WIDTH=200>Hola!</TH>
<TR><TD BGCOLOR="666600" HEIGHT=200
WIDTH=200
ALIGN=middle>You</TD><TD BGCOLOR="996666"
HEIGHT=200 WIDTH=200 ALIGN=middle>Me</TD>
</TABLE>
</CENTER>
</BODY>
</HTML>
```

① The **<CENTER>** tag instructs the table to be centered in the page.

② The **<TABLE>** tag establishes the beginning of the table command. The **BORDER** attribute assigns a 1-pixel default size embossed border to the table.

③ **TR** initiates a table row. **TH** stands for table header. Everything within the **<TH>** tag will automatically be bold and centered. The **BGCOLOR** attribute allows a color to be established within the table cell and can be specified by using hexadecimal color or color names. The **<HEIGHT>** and **<WIDTH>** tags assign dimensions to the table cells by using pixel-based measurements. The **ALIGN=middle** attribute centers the text within the table cells.

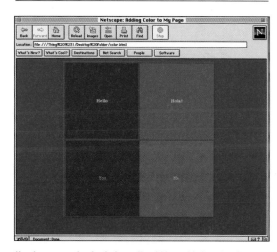

Here's an example of coloring cells within a table by using the BGCOLOR attribute within the <TABLE> tag.

preparing web graphics

creating browser-safe artwork

After seeing what unwanted dithering looks like, it's time to move on to the subject of creating artwork that will not fall prey to the pitfalls of cross-platform inconsistencies. There's a difference between illustration-based artwork and photographic-based artwork. Illustration-based artwork (also known as line art) consists of logos, cartoons, drawings, and graphics that have areas of solid color.

Illustration-based artwork will always compress best in the GIF file format (see Chapter 3, "Web File Formats," and Chapter 4, "Speedy Web Graphics"). The GIF file format is an 8-bit file format, meaning that it already forces you to save images in 256 colors or less. Any 8-bit color format works with color lookup tables, which is often abbreviated using the acronym CLUT. JPEGs do not use CLUTs because they are a 24-bit file format.

I have a CLUT for the browser-safe colors available on my web site (✎ ftp://luna.bearnet.com/pub/lynda/) that can be used by many different imaging programs. You will find the file names and locations listed in the following sections within this chapter. By storing the browser-safe CLUT in a handy place, you can use it to load the 216 colors into paint programs and paint with the colors to ensure that your artwork will not unexpectedly dither.

It's always best to create artwork initially in browser-safe colors, rather than rely on converting the colors afterward. It's rare that you can successfully convert colored artwork to browser-safe artwork with good quality results.

In order to paint, type, and fill with browser-safe colors, first load them into your paint program. Use the eyedropper to select from this color range, and your resulting artwork will be browser safe!

warning

Converting to Browser Safe

There may be times when you have an existing color image that you want to convert to browser-safe colors. It's very rare for an image to look good when a CLUT with colors different from the image has been applied. Photoshop determines how to substitute the new colors, and it might not be yield the results you expected. It's always best to create artwork with browser-safe colors first and not rely on post-processing techniques to fix existing artwork.

step-by-step

Loading a Browser-Safe Swatch Palette into Photoshop

The file bclut2.aco is available from my ftp site:  ftp://luna.bearnet.com/pub/lynda/. It can be loaded into the Photoshop Swatch palette by following these steps.

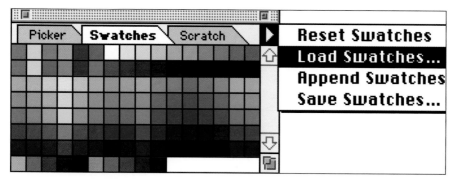

☞ **1**   Choose Windows, Palettes, Show Swatches. Using the upper right arrow, choose Load Swatches from the pull-down menu.

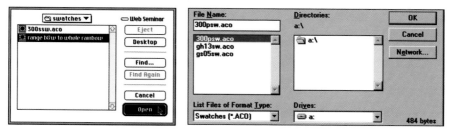

☞ **2**   Select any file with an .aco extension. (ACO is the file format for Photoshop swatch palettes). The custom swatch set appears as a new set in Photoshop's Swatch Palette.

113

remaining browser safe

If you work with browser-safe colors when you create artwork, you still have the important task of ensuring that those colors remain browser safe during the file format conversion and saving process.

Unfortunately, files that are converted to JPEGs do not retain precise color information. The lossy compression method used throws away information, and unfortunately some of that information has to do with color control. Because of this, there is no way to accurately control color using the JPEG file format.

Chapter 3, "Web File Formats," emphasized that JPEGs are not good for graphics. Not only do they compress graphics poorly, but they introduce artifacts into images, which alters color information.

What this means is that you cannot accurately match foreground GIFs to background JPEGs or foreground JPEGs to background GIFs. Even if you prepare images in browser-safe colors, they will not remain browser safe when converted to JPEG, no matter what you do. This is one more reason not to use JPEGs when dealing with flat-style illustration, logos, cartoons, or any other graphical image that would not lend itself to having unwanted dithering. Note: If you use the highest quality JPEGs, color inconsistency can be avoided, but you will suffer larger file sizes. Seems like if one thing doesn't get you, something else does!

Here's an example of a solid browser-safe color, with the hex readout of 51, 153, 153.

When saved as a GIF file, this color stayed browser safe.

When saved as a JPEG, the color shifted from 51, 153, 153 to 154, 154, 156. It is no longer browser safe, as evidenced by the dither when displayed in Netscape under 8-bit monitor conditions.

removing unnecessary colors

At times you will apply the browser-safe palette to a file in order to ensure that the colors within honor the 216-color limit. The problem is that you may want to later reduce the file size even further than 216 by reducing the number of colors.

The example below shows how to apply a browser-safe palette and reduce the color depth.

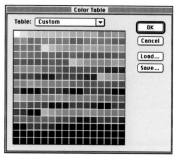

The image is now browser safe, but it is also 216 colors! That's a few too many colors than are necessary for this image. By leaving the image this way, it would be 6.8k.

Bruce Heavin created an illustration in colors other than browser safe.

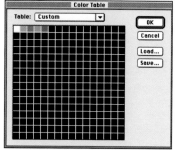

He converted them to browser-safe colors by choosing Image, Mode, Index Color and then loading the 216 browser-safe CLUT file (called bclut2.aco) from my ftp site. Note that in Photoshop 4.0 there is a built-in 216-color table, called Web, that you can select from the Table, pull-down menu.

There's no reason for the image to include all 216 colors. By changing the image back to RGB mode and then back to Indexed Color mode, Bruce chose Exact Palette the second time. This image needs to be assigned only 7 colors! When saved as a GIF with only 7 colors, the image is 5.8k, a 14% file size savings that doesn't affect visual image quality in the least.

Don't Save Browser-Safe Colors in 16-Bit!

Unexpected problems occur when working with browser-safe color. Sometimes browser-safe colors that you thought you set up properly turn out to not be browser safe when you check on them later. What causes this?

One of the main reasons may have something to do with your computer's current bit depth. When you select browser-safe color in thousands of colors, the colors are no longer browser safe! For some unknown reason, browser-safe colors aren't represented by thousands of colors systems. The only solution to this problem is to work in 256 colors or millions of colors while selecting and saving with browser-safe color.

You may be thinking that if the 216 browser-safe colors don't work properly in thousands of colors, you'll have a new set of headaches for users who are viewing your site in thousands of colors (16-bit) mode. Fortunately, this is not the case. The 65,000 colors (16-bit) have enough colors so that the subtle dithering is virtually undetectable.

However, if you create your browser-safe artwork with your computer set to Thousands of Colors and the resulting nonbrowser-safe artwork is viewed in a 256-color environment, the dithering is very noticeable. The moral of this warning is to make sure your authoring system is set to 256 or millions of colors when creating browser-safe artwork. I cannot explain technically why this is happening, but this solution will always work.

vector-based software

Most vector-based software packages were designed for print mediums, not the screen-based web. For this reason, many vector-based programs support only CMYK, not RGB color. Instructions for how to deal with this problem in CorelDRAW, FreeHand, and Illustrator, follow.

Working with CorelDRAW

At the time this chapter was written, the current shipping version of CorelDRAW supported the capability to output files in RGB. The only problem was that it didn't allow you to specify the palette. The next version, 7.0, promises to allow custom palette assignments. It's best to create artwork in CorelDRAW that is close to the colors you want to use and then bring the artwork into Photo-Paint to convert the colors to the browser-safe CLUT. The Photo-Paint 216 palette is called 216clut.cpl. and is available from my ftp site at (✎ ftp:// luna.bearnet. com/pub/lynda/).

Working with FreeHand

Artists who use FreeHand for its excellent type-handling tools and vector-drawing tools are in luck! FreeHand allows users to work directly in RGB and will support the 216 palette.

FreeHand works with RGB percentages rather than specific RGB values. It's possible to mix browser-safe colors right in RGB within FreeHand. Just remember these conversions:

%	rgb	hex
100%	255	FF
80%	204	CC
60%	153	99
40%	102	66
20%	51	33
0%	0	0

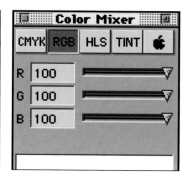

Working with Adobe Illustrator

Adobe Illustrator is an extremely useful program that does many things better than Photoshop. Some of the reasons to use Illustrator are its better handling of text, and its capability to position artwork accurately and create object-oriented artwork that is resolution independent.

The only problem in using Illustrator for web graphics is that it works only in CMYK. It's impossible to load the browser-safe color chart or swatch sets into a CMYK environment. Most artists who use Illustrator for browser-safe color artwork create the artwork in black and white in Illustrator and then import the artwork into Photoshop, where they use the browser-safe swatches.

Note: version 6.0 of Illustrator will let you save GIF files and convert them to a specified palette, including one that contains the 216 browser-safe colors.

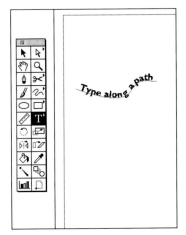

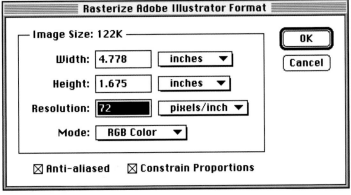

When you open the file in Illustrator, you'll be prompted to rasterize the artwork. This converts the artwork from the Illustrator vector format to the Photoshop bitmap format.

Illustrator is a popular software program because of its superior type handling, accurate positioning features, and resolution-independent drawing tools. Unfortunately it works only in CMYK color, so it's impossible to author web color images directly. Create artwork in black and white first and then save it as a native Illustrator file.

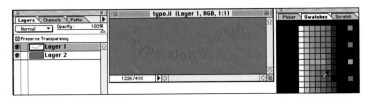

After the artwork is rasterized in Photoshop, it can be painted with the browser-safe color swatches, just like artwork that originated in Photoshop.

color picker-based applications

On the Mac, certain programs don't let you mix colors by percentages or RGB values. A few such programs include Adobe PageMill, Claris Homepage, and BBEdit, which all rely on the Apple Color Picker to choose custom colors.

Pantone has come to the rescue with a Mac-only product called ColorWeb ( http://www. pantone.com). Its Internet-safe color-picking system includes two components: a printed swatch set, and a system Color Picker that displays the 216 safe colors inside the Apple Color Picker dialog box.

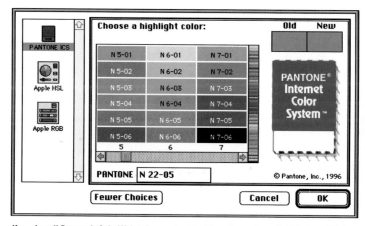

The Pantone Internet Color Guide looks like a typical Pantone color swatch book, except that it has a web-color spin. It profiles and organizes the 216 browser-safe colors in chromatic order and lists the values for RGB, CMYK, hexadecimal, and hexachrome (their proprietary color format for picking printing ink colors).

If you install Pantone's ColorWeb software, it will add another entry, called Pantone ICS, into the Apple Color Picker choices. Pantone ICS will enable you to pick from the 216 browser-safe colors.

warning

CMYK and RGB Compatibility

It should be noted that there is no perfectly accurate way with which to convert CMYK values to RGB. The numbers that the Pantone Internet Color Guide cites for CMYK Internet-safe values are ballpark approximations and do not yield browser-safe colors when converted to RGB. The two color spaces—RGB and CMYK—do not share common colors consistently. Some RGB colors are outside of the CMYK color gamut, and there is nothing anyone can adjust for to create a reliable conversion method.

The ColorWeb software is an excellent (Mac-only) tool that offers the capability to pick browser-safe colors in programs that do not support RGB decimal or RGB percentage-based values. Pricing and order information is available at the Pantone web site ( http://www.pantone.com).

browser-safe photographs?

It's not necessary to save photographs using browser-safe colors. Photographic artwork is also sometimes referred to as "continuous-tone." It can include photos, blurry artwork, glows, and drop shadows.

When an end user on a 256-color system sees a photograph on a web page, the browser converts it to its respective system palette. The good news is that the browser does just as good a job as you could have if you had prebuilt the photograph in the 216 palette. Let the browser do your dirty work for you! Not only will it save time, but if you create photographic artwork in millions, thousands, or adaptive colors, it will look best to end users who have better color systems.

If you are saving your photograph as a JPEG, you do not need to worry about which palette to save it with. JPEGs don't use palettes or CLUTs; they can display any of 16.7 million colors. If you are saving your image as a GIF, you should use an adaptive palette. An adaptive palette chooses colors from the image rather than fixed colors from an unrelated color scheme.

Here's an example of a 24-bit JPEG image. Photographs will always look best as JPEGs.

Here's an example of the same image saved as an 8-bit GIF with an adaptive palette.

Here's the same photograph with the 216 web palette applied to it. It looks the worst of all these examples.

Notice how the adaptive palette has pulled colors from the image?

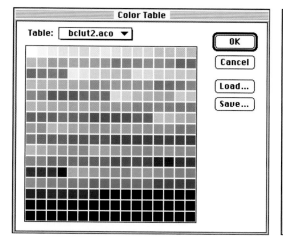

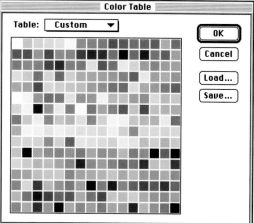

The web palette has its own colors, which don't necessarily relate to the image it has been applied to.

The point that these examples demonstrate is that the web palette doesn't look good on photographs. Those with 8-bit displays will have to see this image with the web palette applied—but why force your end users who have better color systems to see the lowest possible quality? Let the web browser do the dirty work of converting your images for 8-bit systems—but prepare your photographs with adaptive palettes or leave them in 24-bit.

summary

Because your images will end up on computer screens rather than printed pages, there is lots to learn about preparing images that will look good across different browsers, platforms, and operating systems. Here is a summary of what this chapter covered:

- Just because you can see images in millions or thousands of colors doesn't mean your web-viewing audience will. Most end users have video cards that support only 256-color displays.

- Browsers use fixed palettes when they display graphics on 256-color systems. If you use colors outside of the fixed palette, your colors might shift or dither.

- With hexadecimal color, such as those specified in HTML for colored links, backgrounds, and tables, if you don't choose from the 216-color palette, the browser will alter the colors you choose.

- With illustrations, if you use colors outside the 216-color range, your images will most likely dither unexpectedly.

- With photographs, browsers do an excellent job of converting the images to 256 colors so there's no reason to use the 216-color palette.

transparent GIFs

If Transparent GIFs (TGIFs) are an unfamiliar term to you, don't worry. I know of no other application for transparent GIFs other than the web, so they're relatively new to everyone. Transparent GIFs are used to create the illusion of irregularly shaped computer files by assigning one color in a graphic to be invisible. This process is also called masking.

Transparent GIFs, technically referred to as GIF89a, support masking. Not all imaging programs let you save graphics in the GIF89a format, so details on how to use the various helper applications, online services, and programs that support this format are included at the end of this chapter.

Transparency is assigned when the file is saved. There is a variety of software applications that enable you to save and define transparency. I'll cover several of them in this chapter. When working with transparent GIFs, there are two things to keep in mind: first, how to properly make art for one-color masking transparency and second, how to use the programs that let you save the artwork in this file format.

note

JPEG or GIF?

It doesn't matter whether your images or tiled background patterns are saved in JPEG or GIF file format. Those decisions should be based on the principles described in Chapter 4, "Speedy Web Graphics." One thing to caution you about: if you are going to use a solid background image and want it to match your solid foreground image, you must use a JPEG background and JPEG foreground, or a GIF background and a GIF foreground. In other words, the file type must match or you will have color shifts between the elements.

preparing web graphics

masking on the web

Transparency is another word for "mask," and masks are often used in computer graphics to make artwork appear in irregular shapes rather than as squares and rectangles. A computer image file by definition is automatically saved in a rectangle. In my humble opinion, way too much artwork on the web is in the shape of rectangles—buttons, pictures, splash screens, menu bars—ugh. Mastering transparency is the only escape!

There are two types of transparency: that which involves masking and that which involves trickery. The easiest way is the trickery method, so let's study that first. Let's say you have a circle and you want it to look like it's free-floating even though it must be inside a rectangular shape. Make the background behind the circle the same color as your web page. When you put the two together, there should be no obvious rectangular border. Sounds simple? It is.

But there's a snag. Matching foreground and background images on the web takes an extra bit of education. This chapter teaches you how to set exact background colors (assuming your end viewer has not changed his or her preferences to override color choices, for which there is nothing you can do) using two HTML-based techniques. One technique involves using hexadecimal code to set a specific background color, and the other requires setting up the HTML to use a solid pattern tile. Step-by-steps will help you understand these two techniques and will show you how to make the irregularly shaped artwork lay on top of colored backgrounds.

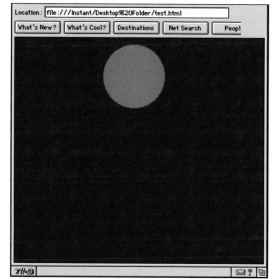

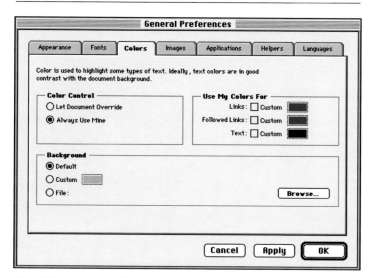

You can easily create the illusion of irregularly shaped images by making the foreground artwork include the same color as your web page's target background.

It's kind of scary for web publishers who count on background colors they pick to achieve the illusion of irregularly shaped images because end viewers can check "Always Use Mine," which will override the color choices specified! If you want to view sites as designers intended them to be seen, make sure "Let Document Override" is always checked instead.

faking transparency the hex way

This technique was covered in Chapter 5, "Cross-Platform Color," but will be reviewed here for the purposes of creating the illusion of transparency. This first example demonstrates how to include irregularly shaped artwork using the <BODY BGCOLOR> tag.

☞ 1   Create artwork that is in an irregular shape. This technique works well on images that include anti-aliasing, soft edges, glows, or drop shadows. Use the eyedropper to find out the RGB values of the image. Hint: If you use the browser-safe color charts in Chapter 5, "Cross-Platform Color," you'll find the hex and RGB colors .

☞ 2   Next, write the following HTML. This code tells the background to be teal blue, by using the hexadecimal code 336666, and inserts the glowingbowler.gif image on the same page.

☞ 1

```
<HTML>
<HEAD>
<CENTER>
<TITLE>Transparency Cheat</TITLE>
</HEAD>
<BODY BGCOLOR=#336666>
</BODY>
<P>
<CENTER>
<IMG SRC="glowingbowler.gif">
</CENTER>
<P>
</HTML>
```

☞ 3   There is no need to use transparency software to achieve this effect. The rectangular image floats over the web page background seamlessly, and creates the illusion of transparency.

☞ 3

creating color with solid patterns

Another way to color the background of a web page is to use a solid color swatch within the background pattern tag, <BODY BACKGROUND>. This tag is more commonly used with artwork that has an image in it, such as a marble texture. The <BODY BACKGROUND> tag takes whatever art you tell it to use and repeats the artwork tiles so that they fill the entire web page.

For instructions on how to make image-filled types of pattern tiles, refer to Chapter 7, "Background Tiles." We are going to use the same HTML technique that Chapter 7 will describe in detail, but our source image for the pattern tile is going to be made out of a solid color instead of an image. As it is repeated over the page, this tile will produce a solid background, identical in appearance to what was demonstrated using the hexadecimal method previously mentioned.

You can actually use both the BGCOLOR and BACK-GROUND attributes inside the same <BODY> tag, which ensures the safest results with this technique. Here's an example of how the code would look:

```
<HTML>
<HEAD><CENTER><TITLE>xxx</TITLE>
</HEAD>
<BODY BGCOLOR=#FFFFCC BACKGROUND="teal.gif">
</BODY> <P>
<CENTER><IMG SRC="glowingbowler.gif">
</CENTER>
<P>
</HTML>
```

It used to be that you might use this method, or this method combined with the previous hexadecimal method, because some browsers didn't support hexadecimal <BGCOLOR> tags. This is no longer the case. One effect you can create is to set up a background color that is a transition effect that precedes a solid color background tile. For example, some people set their hex background to load first with white and then change to black after the solid background tile loads so that they can create an eye-catching flashing effect.

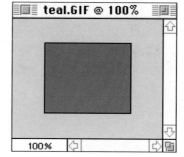

Here's an example of a Photoshop file that is filled with the same solid teal used in the last example. If this image were used as the <BODY BACKGROUND> file, the HTML could not be overridden—regardless of whether someone changed the background color defaults in their browser preferences.

how not to fake transparent artwork

I recommend using transparent GIFs only on web pages that have pattern backgrounds (see Chapter 7, "Background Tiles") because you can create the same effect against solid colors by using the techniques described earlier in this chapter. Establishing transparency in a GIF adds a lot of extra steps in production, so there's no reason to do that when there's an easier way.

The reason I recommend transparency with pattern background tiles is because you can't reliably match a fore-ground image to a background tile in standard HTML. (This is described in detail in Chapter 11, "Alignment.") If you want to put irregularly shaped artwork over patterned backgrounds, you'll have to use transparency.

Here's the same artwork against a pattern. It looks cool!

Unfortunately, if I simply place the precomposited image over a background tile, they don't line up. And to make matters worse, the alignment is offset differently on Mac and PC browsers! The only solution is to make a transparent GIF (the technique of faking transparency shown earlier in this chapter will not work).

making clean transparent artwork

The key to producing effective transparent GIFs is ensuring that your art is produced correctly. We need to begin by first going through a short primer on aliased versus anti-aliased artwork. Anti-aliasing is the process of blending around the edges of a graphic to hide the jagged square pixels it is made of.

Many of the transparent GIFs I see on the web have ugly residual matte lines, which look like colored halos. These matte lines can be traced back to the way in which the image was anti-aliased.

When viewed against black, the image to the lower right has a green halo around it. Why? It was originally created against a teal green background, and its anti-aliased edges still are blending to that color. The transparency only removed the single color teal, and couldn't eliminate the fringe.

Anti-aliasing was designed to hide the fact that computer graphics are made of square, jagged pixels. Computer screens are a pixel-based medium, so the compulsion to hide this fact in print and other media is not necessary for computer screen-based design, such as the web and other multimedia delivery systems such as CD-ROMs. Low-resolution web graphics are much more forgiving of aliasing than their print graphic counterparts.

On the web, anti-aliasing is not always the best approach. Creating clean transparent GIFs is one of those exceptions where aliased graphics create the least amount of problems.

The anti-aliased blended edge is precisely what causes fringing problems once the graphic is converted to a transparent GIF. Because transparent GIFs drop only one color out of your image, you will see all the remaining colors along the blended edge of anti-aliased artwork, even when what you really want is

for all of them to disappear. The only way to avoid this would be for the GIF file format to support masking for more than one color. (Photoshop and PICT file formats, for example, let you mask with 256 levels of transparency, whereas transparent GIFs let you mask with only one.)

Anti-aliasing is the process in which one color and shape blend to another in order to hide the jagged square-pixel nature of computer graphics. You don't notice the anti-aliasing in the reduced (100%) view, but the close-up (400%) shows the blended lines.

Because the original image was created against green, the anti-aliased edge retains a blended green influence. This is the reason behind halo problems in web transparency.

glows, edges, shadows

Because of the problems anti-aliasing introduces, artwork with glows, soft edges, and drop shadows can look awful as transparent GIFs. One popular solution is to build artwork against the same color background that it will be seen against in the web browser. The artwork will look terrible when you make it, but it will look fine once laid against the final background in a web browser.

aliased

anti-aliased

with glow

This figure shows three types of edges for artwork: aliased, anti-aliased, and with a glow.

aliased

anti-aliased

glow

When the different examples of edges are made into transparent GIFs using 1-color transparency, notice how every example except the aliased top version picked up the background color they were made against. That's because the images with soft edges picked up parts of the white color they were created against. This created an unsightly problem, which in the industry is commonly called a halo, fringe, or matte line.

aliased

anti-aliased

with glow

Here's an example of the identical artwork with anti-aliased, shadowed, and blurry edges against the same color background as the target pattern color.

aliased

anti-aliased

glow

When the transparency is set, the files look pretty terrible. They won't look good again until they are laid over a purple background. If prepared this way, you will correct their predisposition to favor any other color, which will eliminate unwanted fringes, halos, and matte lines.

aliased

anti-aliased

glow

The end result looks quite acceptable now. Look ma, no matte lines!

photoshop tips for aliased images

In the following sections, we'll look at how to create artwork for transparent GIFs with aliased edges. An aliased edge has no blended artwork, so there's no possiblity for fringing, halos, or matte lines (different words for the same unwanted effect!).

Photoshop was designed as a sophisticated graphics editing program, and working with aliased tools is foreign to most Photoshop users. Understanding which types of tools are appropriate for the job and how to configure them so that they don't anti-alias is key to mastering clean-edged TGIFs. There are a few different types of graphics we'll study: illustrations, scanned illustrations, and scanned photographs.

Illustration-Based Artwork for Transparent GIFs

If you're an illustrator, you're used to creating artwork from scratch. It's best to start with the correct tools for the job—and they'll most likely be tools you don't normally use. Most paint programs default to working with anti-aliased brushes and fill tools. To create aliased graphics in Photoshop, you want to use the Pencil tool and the Paint Bucket tool to draw and fill shapes.

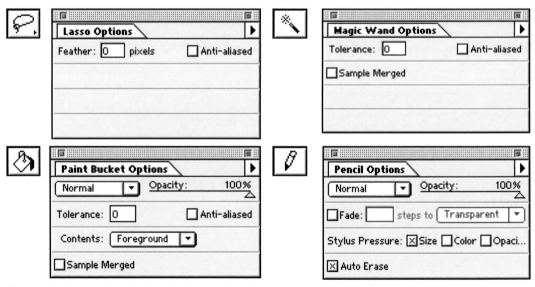

These are the aliased graphic tools of the trade: the lasso, the magic wand, the paint bucket, and the pencil.

While creating your illustrations, be sure to fill the areas that are going to go transparent with a different color. Here's an example of how my logo was prepared for conversion to a transparent GIF. I used an aliased pencil tool with my pressure sensitive tablet to achieve the handwritten font.

It looks like my logo is set against black, but the black is there only so it would be easy to identify when I made this graphic transparent.

Once my logo is transparent and against a background, no one ever has to know it was created against black. It has no residual matte line because the artwork is aliased instead of anti-aliased.

The techniques reviewed here, using the aliased bucket and pencil tools, work great if you're creating flat illustration artwork directly on the computer. But what if you're not? The next section addresses other techniques for converting graphics to TGIFs.

HTML for Transparent GIFs

The HTML for transparent GIFs is identical to the HTML for any other type of GIF or JPEG. The <IMG SRC> tag is all that is needed.

For an **unlinked** transparent GIF graphic, here's the HTML:

```
<IMG SRC="transgif.gif">
```

For a **linked** transparent GIF graphic, here's the HTML:

```
<A HREF="http://www.destination_domain_name.com">
<IMG SRC="transgif.gif"></A>
```

Photo Sources for Transparent GIFs

A common challenge you'll run up against is when you have photographs or existing color illustrations with anti-aliased edges that you want to change to transparent GIFs. You don't have to change the interior of your graphic to be aliased, just the edges. For best results you can work large and use the Magnifying Glass tool to zoom way in to accurately erase the edge using the aliased "block" Eraser tool. You also can use the aliased Lasso tool to select the parts you want to delete. Just make sure the anti-aliased box is unchecked! The edge will look terrible in Photoshop, but will look much better on the web!

If you would like to try this at home, download the dancer.gif file from my ftp server (✍ ftp://luna.bearnet.com /pub/lynda). Here's a step-by-step demonstration of how to make this photograph transparent: the following examples show the correct method to properly prepare photo-based source material for TGIFs.

☞ 1   Scan the photo. Remember to use the correct scale for the web—72 dpi, RGB color, and small dimensions!

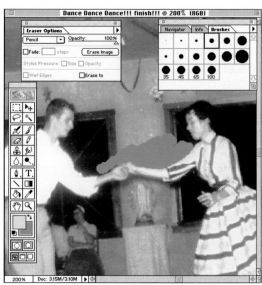

☞ 2   Use the Eraser tool, with the Pencil selected in the pop-up menu. Choose a color that is not in the image itself, so that the color can later be assigned to disappear.

☞ 3 Trace around the shape of the dancing figures. When finished, this image, by itself, will probably look jaggy and horrible around the edges.

☞ 4 Save the image as a transparent GIF and put it on a web page (by following the directions later in this chapter). Notice how the image looks perfectly acceptable once laid over a pattern background? Also, notice the lack of matte lines.

Transparent GIF URLs

Here are some useful URLs to track down transparency tricks and tips:

✎ **Online Transparent GIF creation**
  ✍ http://www.vrl.com/Imaging/invis.html

✎ **Thomas Boutell's WWW FAQ on Transparency**
  ✍ http://sunsite.unc.edu/boutell/faq/tinter.htm

✎ **Chipp Walter's Excellent GIF Transparency Tutorial**
  ✍ http://204.96.160.175/IGOR/photosho.htm

Adobe Photoshop GIF89a Export Plug-In

Current versions of Photoshop ship with a GIF89a plug-in that supports transparency and interlacing. This plug-in works on Mac and Windows versions of Photoshop. This plug-in is pre-installed in current versions of Photoshop. Here's a step-by-step tour through Photoshop's GIF89a plug-in features:

☞ **1**   Open the document you wish to make transparent.

☞ **2**   Convert the file from RGB to Index Color. Go to Image, Mode, select Index, and leave it at its defaults. Or you can practice some of the principles described in Chapter 4, "Speedy Web Graphics." Test the image in 100 colors, or 50, or whatever works. You can decide how low to take the bit depth; the lower you take it, the smaller the file size will be.

☞ **3**   Under File, select Export, GIF89a. Using the Eyedropper tool, click on the areas you want transparent. The preview shows you what you need to see. When finished selecting with the eyedropper, click OK to save.

 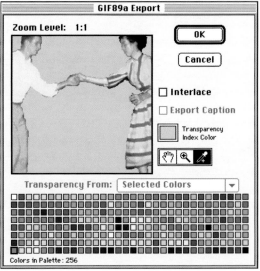

☞ **4**   You set whichever color(s) you wish to disappear with the Eyedropper tool in the GIF89a Photoshop plug-in. I usually uncheck the Interlace box because I am not particularly fond of interlaced images.

online

For those who like to work and surf at the same time, you can make transparent GIFs online over the World Wide Web! There are several sites that will convert a regular GIF into a transparent GIF while you wait. These sites look for an URL that includes a GIF image and will convert the image to the GIF89a format. Some sites let you choose black, white, or an RGB value to go transparent, and others let you click on the image to choose the spot.

To use the online transparency service, you have to give the URL of your image, not the URL of an HTML document. A correct URL would look like this:

✍ http://www.myprovider.com/mysitename/ imagetoconvert.gif

Remember, your artwork must be loaded on a server and be a valid URL.

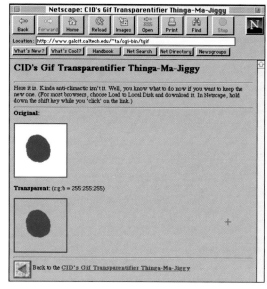

Here's an example of what online transparency software can do. Woo hoo!

 tip

URLs for Online Transparency

✎ **Fefe's Transparency Apparatus**

✍ http://www.inf.fu-berlin.de/~leitner/trans/english.html

✎ **Caltech Logo Tutorial**

✍ http://www.caltech.edu/www/logoinfo.html

✎ **TransWeb**

✍ http://www.mit.edu:8001/transweb.html

✎ **GIF Transparentifier**

✍ http://olympia.ucr.edu/~davec/trans.html

summary

This chapter covered the complex decisions of transparency creation. Here's a summary of key points:

- If you create artwork against solid colors and match the same solid color to your web page background, you can fake transparency. This method is just as effective as creating a transparent GIF, but a lot easier! The only time transparent GIFs are recommended is when you want to put an irregularly shaped image on top of a patterned background tile.

- If you create the transparent artwork with anti-aliased edges, it will be predisposed to work with the colored background it was created against. This often causes unwanted fringing or halos around transparent artwork.

- Creating aliased edges is the key to making transparent artwork look good against any background color or pattern. Learn to create artwork with aliased tools to accomplish this.

- There are many different software packages available from which to create transparent GIFs. Additionally, you will find URLs (listed in this chapter) of online transparency software, which can convert graphics for you while you're online.

making tiles

Making full-screen, wall-to-wall graphics on the web would seem an impossible feat given the slow modems and teeny weeny phone lines most of us have to squeeze connections through. Not to mention the fact that full-screen graphics can mean one thing to a compact portable computer user and another to someone with a 21" monitor! You might think it would take way too long to download an image that fills a viewer's browser screen and that it would be irresponsible to prepare images of this size for web graphics.

Repeated, tilable background patterns are the answer. This chapter covers an HTML tag called <BODY BACK-GROUND>, which allows a single small image to be repeated endlessly so that it fills an entire web page, regardless of size. These single small images will be referred to in this chapter as tiled background patterns. They have the advantage of being small, so they load fast, and they include the capability to repeat over the size of whatever web screen they appear on. Because a small graphic loads faster than a big one, this technique works well to cover a lot of real estate on a web page without incurring a lot of overhead in downloading time.

Background Tiles 7

139

tiling backgrounds

The <BODY BACKGROUND> tag enables the browser to repeat a small graphic and turn it into a full-screen graphic. It accomplishes this effect by taking a single image and tiling it, creating a repeating image that will fill any size screen regardless of computer platform and browser area. The browser needs to load only a single source file for the pattern, and once it's downloaded, it fills the entire web page. This saves time because the wait time is for a single small image, even though the result is that the entire screen fills with an image. Repeated tiles are a great solution for creating full-screen graphics for low-bandwidth delivery systems such as the web.

 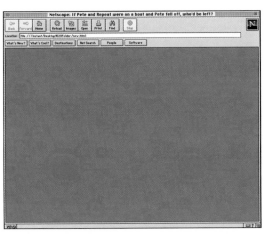

Bandwidth limitations aren't the only problem that tiled background patterns solve. One of the great frustrations most web designers share is HTML's inability to allow for images to be layered. If you consider that layering is a main feature of programs such as Photoshop, QuarkXPress, and PageMaker, you willl understand why this feature in HTML is sorely missed.

HTML allows text, links, and images to go on top of tiled backgrounds, making it an extremely useful and economical design element. The HTML code for this tiling effect is quite simple. The real challenge is making the art look good and controlling whether the seams of each repeated image are obvious or invisible.

determining tiled pattern sizes

One of the first questions that comes to mind is how big the tiled image should be. HTML puts no restrictions on the size of a source for a background tile. The image has to be square or rectangular, however, because that's the native shape of any computer file.

The size of the image is entirely up to you. You should realize that the size of a tile is going to dictate how many times it repeats. If a viewer's monitor is 640×480 pixels and your tile is 320×240, it will repeat 4 times. If it were 20×20 pixels, it would repeat 32 times.

Be aware, however, that file size restrictions must still be honored. If you create a tile that takes up a lot of memory, it will take the same amount of time to load as any other kind of huge graphic you put on the web. If need be, refer back to Chapter 4, "Speedy Web Graphics," for methods to minimize file sizes.

Source File

Result

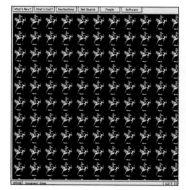
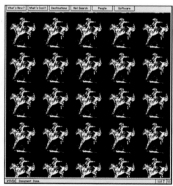
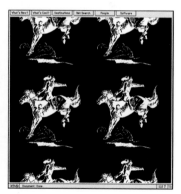

The number of repeats of a tiled background image is dependent on whether a small, medium, or large source file is used.

full-screen body backgrounds?

Why would you use an image with large pixel dimensions as a tiled background since it seems to defeat the point? Because it could go behind other images and text, making a full-screen backdrop for other images on your page. HTML doesn't easily let you put text or images over regular images. The easiest way around this restriction is to use a background tiled graphic.

Here's the full-screen (800×600 pixel) graphic that Bruce used on a web page (now extinct) for *The Net* magazine. It is only 11.6k because there are very few colors in this image.

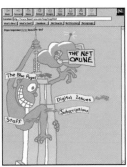

With other images laid over the full-screen background, this is an effective and economical use of a large background tile.

An example of a 24.7k JPEG image used as a background for Art Center's site (✎ http://www.artcenter.edu).

Combined with HTML text, this page looks rich and layered, and is not too large to download.

file formats for patterned tiles

GIFs and JPEGs are the standard file formats for the web, and tiled patterns are no exception. Just remember to follow the kilobyte rule. Every kilobyte of file size represents 1 second of download time to your viewer. The full size of the background pattern gets added to the download! If you have a background that's 60k and two images that are 10k each, the total file size of your page will be 80k. You would have just added a minute of download time to your page! Therefore, tiled backgrounds that take up a lot of memory are extra annoying to your audience during download.

Be careful if you are trying to match foreground and background tile images. They must both be the same file format—GIF and GIF or JPEG and JPEG—if you want the colors to match perfectly.

As usual, always save your file names in lowercase and use the extensions .jpg or .gif to let the HTML code know what kind of image it has to load. I usually put the word "pat" somewhere in a pattern file name, just for my own reference. That way I know what I intended to use the file for when searching for it in a text list, such as my server directory.

HTML code for background tiles

HTML for Tiles

It is simple to include a patterned background in an HTML document. Here's the bare minimum code:

```
<HTML>
<BODY BACKGROUND="pat.gif">
</BODY>
</HTML>
```

1 The **<BODY BACKGROUND>** tag enables you to add a background tile to the page. The "**pat.gif**" is the name of the image being tiled in this example.

HTML for Tiles and Foreground Image

If you want to have an image lay over a background, the code would look like this:

```
<HTML>
<BODY BACKGROUND="pat.gif">
<IMG SRC="smoke.gif">
</BODY>
</HTML>
```

1 The **<IMG SRC>** tag enables you to include an image that will lay over the background tile.

pat.gif

smoke.gif

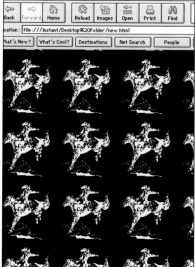

The final result of using the <BODY BACKGROUND= "pat.gif"> tag.

The finished web page with the <IMG SRC="smoke.gif"> tag.

seams or no seams?

The next sections take a look at two different ways to present your background tile on your web page: with or without seams.

Seams

When an image has obvious seams, it looks tiled on purpose. Some web pages look great wallpapered with an obvious border. Andy Warhol shocked the art world in the 1960s and first earned his notoriety by making images of repeating soup cans on a single canvas. Video walls are often built on the power of images repeating in squares. There's nothing wrong with making patterns that have obvious borders and repeats, especially if that's what you have in mind. Making a tiled pattern with an obvious repeating border is fairly simple.

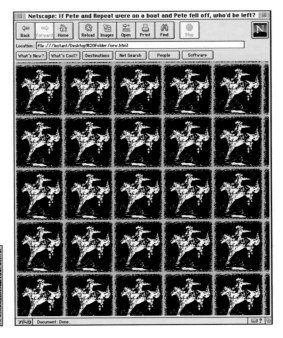

No Seams, the Photoshop Way

When "seamless" patterns are described, it means the border of the pattern tile is impossible to locate. There aren't any pros or cons to using seamless or seamed tiles; it's purely an aesthetic decision. Seamless tiles, however, are much trickier to make.

Here's a step-by-step example of how Bruce Heavin, using Photoshop, makes his seamless pattern artwork.

☞ 1   Bruce began by drawing the stars in a corner of this 400×400, 72 dpi file.

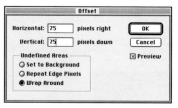

☞ 2   Using the Offset filter in Photoshop (under Filter, Other, Offset), Bruce entered the settings 75 pixels right, with 75 pixels down, using the Wrap Around method.

☞ 3   The setting Bruce entered in the Offset filter caused the image to shift position.

☞ 4   Bruce reapplied the Offset filter to fill in the holes in the image that became visible.

☞ 5   Here is the finished tile. Without the Offset filter, Bruce would have never been able to see the edges of this image in order to design them so that they wouldn't show.

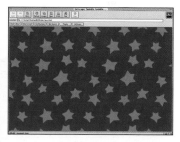

☞ 6   Once the filter was finished, Bruce used the Magic Wand, at a tolerance of 1, to select the white in the image. He filled it with a browser-safe teal color.

aesthetics of backgrounds

Always pay attention to contrast and value (lights and darks) when creating background tiles. If you have a light background, use dark type. If you have a dark background, use light type. If you have both darks and lights in a background, neither light nor dark type will work consistently against them. This is a basic, simple rule to follow, and your site will avoid the pitfalls of poor background tile aesthetics. Using either all dark values or all light values seems like common sense, but tour the web a bit and you'll soon see rainbow-colored back-grounds with unreadable black type everywhere.

Make sure your images read. I don't mean your tiles should go to school to learn phonetics—instead I'm talk-ing about readability of image versus background. The examples of the bronco tile have great contrast and "read" as a horse image, but the second you try to put type over them, they will not "read" anymore.

When the background is black and white, nothing reads well on top of it.

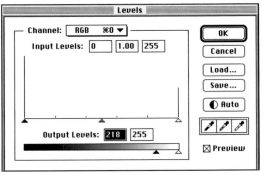

Using the Adjust Levels, Output Levels in Photoshop, it's possible to lighten or darken the overall contrast of the image.

While it might seem obvious, light and medium value colors will read over a dark background.

With a light background, the reverse is true. It's not enough to make a cool looking background tile—always check to make sure your type reads over it as well! If it doesn't read, make the necessary adjustments to the type color or contrast of the background image.

other tricks

When background tiles load, they usually do so in one fell swoop, where you don't notice which direction they're loading from. This is not the case, however, if you make really skinny background tiles.

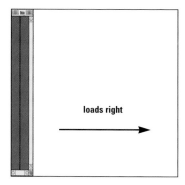

loads right

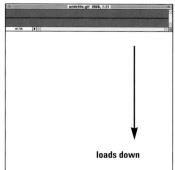

loads down

The vertical tile will load left to right and the horizontal tile will load top to bottom. They look like animated wipes. These images are only one pixel wide or high. Warning: while this effect is interesting the first time around, it can be very annoying on slow connections or on a page that is visited frequently.

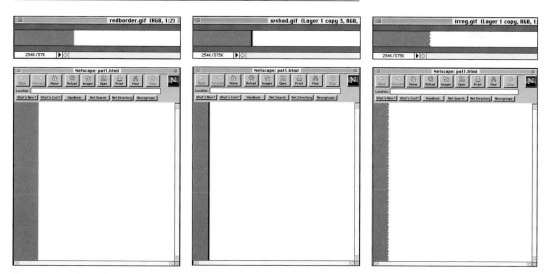

You can also design background images so that they have runners going down their left side. These are some examples of the source images and the resulting effect they have in the browser window.

summary

Background tiles are a great asset to most web pages. There are a lot of factors that go into making effective tiles. Here's a list of some of the possibilities:

✎ Background tiles are one way to fill a web page with visual content without taking up a lot of memory and downloading time.

✎ Choosing whether to make tiles that have visible seams or not is an aesthetic decision that is dependent on the content of your page.

✎ There is no "right" size for a background tile. The size simply will dictate the number of repeats.

✎ Be sure to pay attention to the "value" (lights and darks) of your web pages. Make dark backgrounds with light text, or light backgrounds with dark text. Don't use high-contrast source material for background tiles.

✎ You cannot reliably match between different file formats. If you are looking to match color, be sure to use a JPEG background tile with a JPEG foreground image, or GIF and GIF. There is no harm in mixing file formats except for unreliable color matching.

navigation

Navigation issues are not present in print design; everyone knows how to navigate through a book or magazine—just turn the pages. But with the web's ability to link graphics and text comes the need to understand a bit about navigation. How does one offer visual design direction to help guide others to information? Some of the navigation issues in web design that this chapter covers are:

- Programming text and images to link

- Turning off borders of linked images

- Creating navigation bars

- Creating imagemaps

- Creating frames

Creating links for text and images involves HTML. Creating images that look like navigational buttons involves design. Creating single images that link to multiple URLs involves HTML and design. Web navigation brings this all together as one artform that combines design, programming, and organizational skills.

identifying hot images

Images that are hot have certain visual markings that are different from inline graphics. Typically, a border appears around an image that links you somewhere else, and this border defaults to a blue color in most browsers. If your audience has had any experience on the web, they will have been trained that any time they encounter a border around an image, it means the image can be clicked on as an active link.

There are some instances where a hot image will not have a telltale border around it. If you'd prefer that your hot graphic be without one, this chapter will describe how to program the border to be "invisible." The only way a viewer will know to click on these types of borderless hot images is if your graphic invites them to bring their cursor closer. In most browsers, when the viewer's cursor passes over a hot spot, it changes from a pointer to the hand cursor. This indicates, just like the border symbol, that an image is a clickable button instead of a static inline graphic.

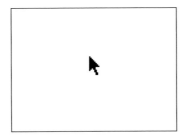

The arrow cursor signifies there is no link.

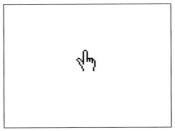

The pointing hand cursor indicates that the text or image is linked (hot).

aesthetic cues for hot images

Many designers, myself included, have grown weary of predictable beveled 3D buttons on web pages. The truth is, however, that beveled 3D buttons give a universally accepted visual cue that a graphic has linking properties. If you're tired of the 3D look, however, there are other signals that imply a linked image. Drop shadows are often used, as are colored shapes. A sample gallery of navigation-style graphics follows. These were created by Bruce Heavin, using the illustration he made of me, with Alien Skin's Black Box Photoshop filters (✍ http://www.alienskin.com). The Alien Skin filters are Mac- and PC-compatible Photoshop filters that save a lot of time and fussing with complicated alpha channel operations.

Cutout

Drop Shadow

Carve

Cutout to Bkgd

Glass

Glow

Inner Bevel

Outer Bevel

MetaTool's site (home of KPT Bryce, PowerTools, and Power Goo) has a lot of playful linked graphics: ✍ http://www. metatools.com/.

Cutout to Image

Drop Shadow

Carve

Cutout to Bkgd Color

Glass

Glow

Inner Bevel

Outer Bevel

These button samples were created with a Photoshop filter set called Black Box, available from Alien Skin Software.

HTML for hot images

Creating Linked Images and Text

The easiest way to create a link that connects one graphic to another web source is to use the <A HREF></A> tag with an <IMG SRC> tag nested inside. This combination of tags automatically defaults to putting a border around the graphic. Here's an example of this standard HTML code.

```
<HTML>
<A HREF="http://www.lynda.com">
<IMG SRC="letsdophone.gif"></A>
</HTML>
```

A linked image often has a telltale blue border, and the cursor will change to a pointing finger when viewed in browsers.

Turning Off Image Borders

Sometimes that pesky blue border around an image is totally wrong for the page it was designed for. If you've gone to a great deal of trouble to make an irregularly shaped image float freely on a background (using techniques described in Chapter 6, "Transparency"), you aren't going to want to ruin the illusion you worked so hard to achieve by having a glaring rectangular shape around your graphic.

Here's the code to eliminate the border.

```
<HTML>
<A HREF="http://www.lynda.com">
<IMG SRC="letsdophone.gif" BORDER=0></A>
</HTML>
```

Here's an example of a linked image with no border. The border was turned off within the HTML, but the pointing finger cursor will still appear when the mouse rolls over the linked image.

Just as you can make the border disappear, you can also make it appear stronger. The following Netscape-specific code gives a thicker border to the image. Notice how the value of the BORDER attribute has changed from 0 to 5.

```
<HTML>
<A HREF="http://lynda.com">
<IMG SRC="letsdophone.gif" BORDER=5></A>
</HTML>
```

This linked image has been programmed to have a thicker border.

Sometimes your page has a specific color theme and the standard blue rectangle doesn't fit in. You can also change the color of your borders if you program the links on your page to include hexadecimal values inside the <BODY LINK> tag (see Chapter 5, "Cross-Platform Color"). This code changes the border color of the current image.

```
<HTML>
<BODY LINK="FFCC00">
<A HREF="http://www.lynda.com">
<IMG SRC="letsdophone.gif" BORDER=5></A>
</BODY>
</HTML>
```

You can change the color of your border by including hexadecimal color values in your code.

navigation bars

Navigation bars can be made out of text or images or both. They provide entranceways to your information. The same HTML tags that were just reviewed apply to navigation bars. Examples follow.

This is the code for the navigation bar at the bottom of my page.

```
<A HREF=/>home</A>
  ¦ <A HREF=/dwg/links.html>links</A>
  ¦ <A HREF=/dwg/multigif.html>a-gifs</A>
  ¦ <A HREF=/hex.html>color</A>
  ¦ <A HREF=/books.html>web design books</A>
  ¦ <A HREF=/dwg/wds.html>classes</A>
<BR>
<A HREF=/articles.html>articles</A>
  ¦ <A HREF=/dwg/vi.html>inspiration</A
  ¦ <A HREF=/dwg/mw.html>macworld</A>
  ¦ <A HREF=http://www.weinman.com/>family</A>
  ¦ <A HREF=/webdesign.html>list</A>
<BR>
<A HREF=/dwg/mg.html>motion graphics</A>
  ¦ <A HREF=http://www.cgibook.com/>cgi</A>
  ¦ <A HREF=/guestbook/>guestbook</A>
  ¦ <A HREF=/bookstore/>bookstore</A>
  ¦ <A HREF=/email.html>e-mail</A>
```

home | links | a-gifs | color | web design books | classes
articles | inspiration | macworld | family | list
motion graphics | cgi | guestbook | bookstore | e-mail

This is what my navigation bar looked like at the time this chapter was written, using straight HTML text. I have so many categories that I decided against icons on my site.

The following HTML for a navigation bar that includes images and text is slightly more complex because it involves tables for placement and font sizing tags.

```
<TABLE BORDER=0 CELLPADDING="3"
CELLSPACING="0">

<TR><TD ALIGN=center><A HREF="art.html">
<IMG SRC="elk.gif" ALIGN=middle BORDER="0"
ALT="Art"></A></TD><TD ALIGN=center>
<A HREF="artists.html"><IMG SRC="horse.gif"
ALIGN=middle BORDER="0"
ALT="Artists"></A></TD><TD ALIGN=center>
<A HREF="life.html"><IMG SRC="buffalo.gif"
ALIGN=middle BORDER="0"
ALT="Life"></A></TD><TD VALIGN=top ALIGN=cen-
ter><A HREF="info.html"><IMG SRC="round.gif"
ALIGN=middle BORDER="0"
ALT="Info"></A></TD><TD ALIGN=center>
<A HREF="us.html"><IMG SRC="sunbird.gif"
ALIGN=middle BORDER="0"
ALT="Us"></A></TD></TR>

<TR><TD ALIGN=center><A HREF="art.html">
<IMG SRC="spot.gif" ALIGN=middle ALT="."
BORDER=0></A></TD><TD ALIGN=center>
<A HREF="artists.html"><IMG SRC="spot.gif"
ALIGN=middle BORDER="0" ALT="."></A></TD>
<TD ALIGN=center><A HREF="life.html">
<IMG SRC="spot.gif" ALIGN=middle ALT="."
BORDER=0></A></TD><TD ALIGN=center><A
HREF="info.html"><IMG SRC="spot.gif"
ALIGN=middle ALT="." BORDER=0></A></TD><TD
ALIGN=center><A HREF="us.html"><IMG
SRC="spot.gif" ALIGN=middle ALT="." BOR-
DER=0></A></TD></TR>

<TR><TD ALIGN=center><FONT SIZE="+2"><TT>
<A HREF="art.html">Art</A></TT></FONT></TD>
<TD ALIGN=center><FONT SIZE="+2"><TT>
<A HREF="artists.html">Artists</A></TT></FONT>
```

```
</TD><TD ALIGN=center><FONT SIZE="+2"><TT>
<A HREF="life.html">Life</A></TT></FONT></TD>
<TD VALIGN=top ALIGN=center>
<FONT SIZE="+2"><TT><A
HREF="info.html">Info</A></TT></FONT></TD>
<TD ALIGN=center><FONT SIZE="+2"><TT>
<A HREF="us.html">Us</A></TT></FONT></TD></TR>
</TABLE>
```

My brother's site (✎ www.weinman.com/wew/) takes the navigation bar idea a step further and uses text and images with a "rollover" technique.

This navigation bar was designed by Ann E. Fullerton and can be found at ✎ http://www.nativespirits.com. This code is much more complex because it involves all kinds of tricks we haven't gotten to yet. (Hint: Try Chapter 10, "Typography," and Chapter 11, "Alignment.")

You don't know what categories the icons represent until your cursor rolls over the artwork, which brings up the text underneath. This was done using JavaScript with two GIF files, one with the text and the other without. You can view the JavaScript source code for this effect at ✎ www.webmonster.net.

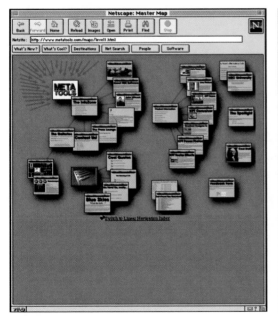

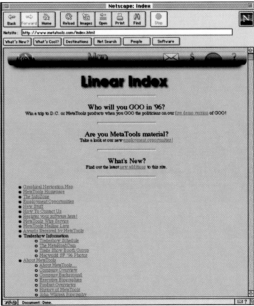

MetaTools has two types of navigation systems on its site: the one on the left, which is image-based, and the one on the right, which is the alternative, text-based page.

what are imagemaps?

At many web sites you will see a list of underlined text links on a page (often referred to as a hotlist). This is simply a list of multiple URLs assigned to multiple text objects. Instead of using multiple text links, however, the list of URLs could be attached to a single image object. Such an object is called an imagemap, which is a fancy way of presenting a list of links. This takes a little longer to download than a hotlist because of the added time required by the graphic to load. Most of the time it's worth the wait because imagemaps are a more convenient, more visual way to present multiple choices to your audience.

This image works well as an imagemap.

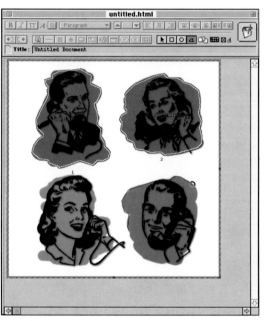

Imagemap software enables you to select regions and assign multiple links to a single image. A list of imagemap software is presented later in this chapter.

client side versus server side

An imagemap must contain specific information, such as coordinates for regions within a single image that are hyperlinked to multiple URLs.

A client-side imagemap requires that all the information about the imagemap be stored within the HTML document. A server-side imagemap requires that the information about the imagemap be saved within a "map definition file" that needs to be stored on a server and accessed by a CGI script. In general, a server-side imagemap is far more complicated to set up than a client-side imagemap. Server-side imagemaps work very differently on different systems—even on different systems using the same brand of server!

Another difference is how the two types of imagemaps display data within the Netscape browser. A server-side imagemap shows the coordinates at the bottom of the screen, whereas a client-side imagemap shows the actual URL at the bottom of the screen, which is much nicer.

Most people prefer client-side imagemaps over server-side imagemaps, but some older browsers still don't support the tags. That's why many webmasters include both types of imagemaps in their documents.

http://www.razorfish.com/bluedot/typo/menu.map?105,70

Here is an example of a server-side imagemap reading on the bottom navigation bar of Netscape. It shows the position coordinates.

http://www.cgibook.com/links.html

Here is an example of a client-side imagemap reading on the bottom navigation bar of Netscape. It shows the URL! Much better.

creating client-side imagemaps

Creating client-side imagemaps is slightly easier than creating server-side imagemaps because you don't need a CGI or a separate map definition file. The steps for creating a client-side imagemap follow:

☞ 1   First, make sure your source graphic is saved as a GIF (standard, transparent, or interlaced will all work) or a JPEG. Don't forget to use the proper extensions: .gif and .jpg in lowercase, with no spaces.

☞ 2   Get the coordinates for the shapes you wish to define as imagemaps within your image. It's possible to get these coordinates in many WYSIWYG HTML editors, and in the two programs mentioned here: MapEdit and WebMap. MapEdit automatically generates the imagemap coordinates in a client-side configuration. WebMap does not, but you can use a converter and have it restructure the data in the necessary fashion. Here's a converter that will help: ✍ http://hyperarchives.lcs.mit.edu/HyperArchive/Archive/text/html/map-convert-10-a.hqx.

☞ 3   The coordinate information needs to be configured differently for a client-side imagemap than for a server-side imagemap. Here is an example of what the client-side coordinate data would look like.

❶ `<MAP NAME="imagemap">`
`<AREA SHAPE="polygon"`
`COORDS="302,152,331,153,349,170,339,193,`
`303,197,277,186,277,172,289,159,302,152"`
❷ `HREF="http://www.stink.com/sketches">`
❸ `<AREA SHAPE="polygon"`
`COORDS="297,87,343,85,363,103,354,130,`
`311,142,277,134,264,118,273,98,297,87"`
`HREF="http://www.stink.com/images/">`
`<AREA SHAPE="polygon"`

`COORDS="302,152,331,153,349,170, 339,193,`
`303,197,277,186,277,172,289,159,302,152`
`"HREF="/www.stink.com/films/">`
❹ `<IMG SRC="imagemap.gif" WIDTH="400"`
`HEIGHT="300"`
❺ `BORDER=0`
❻ `USEMAP="#imagemap" ISMAP>`
❼ `</MAP>`

Everything within the client-side imagemap information gets stored within the HTML. This makes the code for client-side imagemaps longer than that of the server-side, which does not include the coordinate data.

❶ The map name is something that you define. It can be any name but must match what is used in the **<MAP NAME>** tag.

❷ The **<HREF>** tag instructs the imagemap to load the referenced HTML.

❸ This part defines which shape the imagemap forms.

❹ Unlike the **CERN** and **NCSA** server-side map definition example, on a client side example no **<A HREF>** tag is necessary. The image for the map is told to display via the **<IMG SRC>** tag.

❺ Just like the server-side example, the **BORDER=0** tag turns off the default blue border. It's not necessary to turn the border off, but it often ruins the illusion of irregularly shaped regions if you leave it turned on.

❻ The **<USEMAP>** tag specifies the name of the client-side imagemap file to use. The **#** character must always precede the map name.

❼ This tag is required to end the client-side imagemap.

158

server-side imagemaps

Imagemaps are more complicated to code than creating single linked images using the <A HREF><IMG SRC></A> tag. They are complicated on a number of fronts. Each hot region's dimensions in pixels have to be determined and documented. In the case of a server-side map, the dimensions must be stored in an imagemap definition file. This definition file is composed slightly differently depending on which kind of server your web site uses.

The server is where your artwork and HTML gets stored. There are two types of servers—NCSA and CERN—and each requires the imagemap definition file code to be slightly different. This means that you have to ensure that the way you've coded the imagemap is compatible with the type of server your site is stored on. The first step to deciding how to build your imagemap is to call the online service provider with whom you have your Internet account and web site to find out what kind of server they use.

Do You Really Need an Imagemap?

Carefully analyze whether you really need an imagemap or if there's some other way to accomplish the same goal. For example, if your image is composed of rectangles, or can be seamed together by using rectangular shapes (or transparent irregular shapes, see Chapter 6, "Transparency "), it may be easier on your end to load multiple single graphics with independent links than to load one graphic with multiple links.

You will see examples of imagemaps used on opening menu screens all over the web. Sometimes an imagemap is used, even when the menu bar is composed of rectangular shapes. Some sites do this because the one image will load faster than multiple images. This is a valid reason to use an imagemap, but even so, the difficulty of creating and maintaining one might outweigh the performance increase. Other sites do it just because they can. Perhaps it's trendy and shows off a certain amount of web-design machismo? I don't know, but it's another decision you get to make when building your site. I, being the lazy sort, often opt for avoiding the imagemap-making task whenever possible.

creating server-side imagemaps

Let's walk through the imagemap-making process quickly and then break out with more detail.

☞ **1** The first step to making an imagemap is to create or choose a graphic as the source for the map. It's easiest to define regions if your graphic has obvious areas, such as a map or illustration, but you can use anything, including photographs and typography.

☞ **2** After you've chosen an image, you will need to create a map definition file—a text file you create that contains information about where the hotspots are located on your image. You can define the regions by using polygons or circles with the location of each region defined by pixels. This information is then composed as a text file specifically prepared for either a CERN or NCSA server.

☞ **3** Next, with a server-side imagemap, a map-processing CGI script is required to instruct the server to recognize the map definition file. Different scripts work for different platforms and servers, and it's best to contact your provider to ask what type of CGI works with their server. Chances are, they already use a CGI script that they'll let you have access to and can instruct you on how to use it properly.

☞ **4** And last, set up the HTML tags to support the imagemap using the <ISMAP> tag.

Now, let's break this down further and walk through the process used to create imagemaps.

Defining the Regions of an Imagemap

Manually defining the coordinates of an imagemap can be a hellacious chore. You need to plot each point and arrive at the x and y coordinates of each region. After you collect all the data, you need to write a text file for the server (slightly different ones for NCSA and CERN servers). This type of grunt work would be best handled by a helper app, and we're lucky that several have cropped up that do the repetitive chore well. This section will show you how to work with two helper apps: WebMap for Mac imagemap authoring and MapEdit for PC imagemap.

Here's an example of what a map definition file looks like for an **NCSA** server.

```
# Created by WebMap 1.0
# Wednesday, November 27, 1996 at 8:52 PM
# Format: NCSA

poly http://www.stink.com/films/ 252,43 275,26
309,21 333,23 340,42 313,68 268,78 248,68
246,48 252,43
poly http://www.stink.com/images/ 297,87
343,85 363,103 354,130 311,142 277,134 264,118
273,98 297,87
poly http://www.stink.com/sketches/ 302,152
331,153 349,170 339,193 303,197 277,186
277,172 289,159 302,152
```

Here's an example of what a map definition file looks like for a **CERN** server:

```
# Created by WebMap 1.0
# Wednesday, November 27, 1996 at 8:52 PM
# Format: CERN

poly http://www.stink.com/sketches/ 302,152
331,153 349,170 339,193 303,197 277,186
```

```
277,172 289,159 302,152
poly http://www.stink.com/images/ 297,87
343,85 363,103 354,130 311,142 277,134 264,118
273,98 297,87
poly http://www.stink.com/films/ 252,43 275,26
309,21 333,23 340,42 313,68 268,78 248,68
246,48 252,43
```

The HTML to Support Server-Side Imagemaps

❶ `<A HREF="http://www.domain.nam/cgi-bin/filename.map">`

❷ `<IMG SRC="imagename.gif"`

❸ `BORDER=0`

❹ `ISMAP>`

❺ `</A>`

❶ This establishes the anchor or destination of the links for the imagemap. Because the map definition file is included in the absolute path, the HTML will reference the imagemap coordinates and the **CGI script**.

❷ This tag defines the name of the image to which the imagemap will be applied.

❸ Whenever there's an **<A HREF>** tag, it automatically generates a default blue border around the graphic. Including the **BORDER=0** tag will turn off the border.

❹ The **ISMAP** command must be included at the end of a server-side imagemap tag.

❺ The **</A>** is required to end the **<A HREF>** tag.

The HTML document must now be loaded to the server with the GIF or JPEG, and the imagemap definition file map with the .map extension. Unlike most HTML, there is no way a server-side imagemap can be tested from your local hard drive. You must upload the proper files to the server first, or the imagemap will not work.

Server-Side with Client-Side Imagemaps

Many people use both server-side and client-side maps. This enables viewers from any browser to be able to use the imagemap.

Here's the code necessary to combine both types of imagemap features.

```
<A HREF="http://www.domain.nam/cgi-bin/
filename.map">
<IMG SRC="imagemap.gif"
BORDER=0
USEMAP="#imagemap"
ISMAP>
<MAP NAME="imagemap">
<AREA SHAPE="polygon"
COORDS="302,152,331,153,349,170,339,193,
303,197,277,186,277,172,289,159,302,152"
HREF="http://www.stink.com/sketches">
<AREA SHAPE="polygon"
COORDS="297,87,343,85,363,103,354,130,
311,142,277,134,264,118,273,98,297,87"
HREF="http://www.stink.com/images/">
</MAP>
<A HREF="http://www.domain.nam/cgi-bin/
filename.map">
<IMG SRC="../credits/credits_b.GIF" WIDTH=160
HEIGHT=116
ALT="credits" BORDER=0
USEMAP="#credits_b" ISMAP>
</A>
<MAP NAME="credits_b">
<AREA SHAPE="polygon"
COORDS="302,152,331,153,349,17
339,193,303,197,277,186,277,172,289,
159,302,152"
<AREA SHAPE="rect" COORDS="2,73,128,97"
HREF="http://www.stink.com/films/">
</MAP>
```

161

Importance of the <ALT> Tag

The <ALT> tag provides alternative information to images that can be read by text-based browsers. Let's say that visitors to your site arrive with browser software that does not recognize imagemaps. Or they've turned off their images because they're in a hurry? Or they're disabled (yes, even visually impaired people can and do use the text-based web; there are devices that can "read" the pages to them). All these situations can be accommodated by adding one simple <ALT> tag to your HTML.

Using our example one more time, here's where the tag would be included.

```
<A HREF="http://www.domain.nam/cgi-bin/
filename.map">
<IMG SRC="imagename.gif" ALT="this is an
image of my bla bla"
BORDER=0
ISMAP>
```

Importance of <WIDTH> and <HEIGHT> Tags

By adding <WIDTH> and <HEIGHT> tags to images within HTML, you are giving the browser information about the size of your graphic. This is a good thing, for a couple of reasons. First, the browser doesn't have to calculate the image size because you've supplied the information for it, which saves time. Also, it allows the text to load before the images, which can be a good thing with large images. Audiences will get something to look at while they're waiting! MSIE actually requires that you use the WIDTH and HEIGHT tag attributes, or the client-side imagemap tags don't even work.

So then, here's the way to implement the HEIGHT and WIDTH tag attributes.

```
<A HREF="http://www.domain.nam/cgi-bin/file-
name.map">
```

```
<IMG SRC="imagename.gif" WIDTH=350 HEIGHT=200
ALT="this is an image of my bla bla"
BORDER=0
ISMAP>
```

The values you put inside the <WIDTH> and <HEIGHT> tags reflect how large the image is, measured by pixels. You can even resize an image if you put values that are larger or smaller than the image! Basically, the browser uses your information for the image size instead of looking to the image itself for size information.

Imagemap Tutorial URLs

- ✐ http://www.ihip.com/
- ✐ http://www.spyglass.com/techspec/ tutorial/img_maps.html

Imagemap Software Tools

- **MapEdit (Windows, PC and Unix)**
  - ✐ http://www.boutell.com/mapedit/

- **MapThis! (Windows)**
  - ✐ http://galadriel.ecaetc.ohio-state. edu/tc/mt/

- **WebMap (Macintosh)**
  - ✐ http://home.city.net/cnx/software/ webmap.html

- **Fleishman's Server-Client Online Converter**
  - ✐ http://www.popco.com/popco/ convertmaps.html

frames for navigation

What are frames? Frames offer the capability to divide a web page into regions so that each region functions as its own web page. This means parts of a page can change, while other regions of the page remain static. Frames are perfect for navigation bars that won't change from page to page, while other content can be set to change independently.

Frames sound great in theory, but there are some noteworthy snags. Many site designers insert existing web pages that were originally designed for full-screen browsers into cramped small-frame regions. This forces the end viewer to scroll through graphics and text inside smaller windows than the pages were originally designed for. Real estate on a web page is already a precious commodity, and breaking apart a small screen into multiple small screens can do more damage to your presentation than good. My recommendation is that you use no more than three frame regions to a page, so that your audience isn't frustrated by having to scroll through small windows.

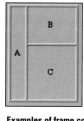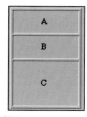

Examples of frame configurations from the excellent tutorial HTML for Angels site in Japan: http://ncdesign.kyushu-id.ac.jp/html/Normal/frame.html.

By clicking on the left-hand frame, content in the right-hand frame updates independently. These examples are from http://www.hotwired.com/cocktail/. **A thorough case-study of this site can be found in my second book, <deconstructing web graphics>.**

HTML for Frames

The HTML for frames is often difficult to understand because it, by nature, includes other "nested" HTML documents. The first document in this example is named framed.html and displays three frame regions. The content of those frames is actually contained in three other HTML documents that this document references. The three other files are named header.html, menu.html, and info.html.

framed.html • The opening page of the sample frameset.

```
<HTML>
<HEAD>
<TITLE>Framed!
</TITLE>
</HEAD>
```
❶ `<FRAMESET ROWS="108,*">`
❷ `<FRAME SRC="header.html" MARGIN-`
`WIDTH=0 MARGINHEIGHT=0 NORESIZE`
`SCROLLING="no"    NAME="header">`
❸ `<FRAMESET COLS="200,*">`
❹ `<FRAME MARGINWIDTH=10 MARGINHEIGHT=10`
`SRC="menu.html" NORESIZE SCROLLING="no"`
`NAME="menu">`

❺ `<FRAME MARGINWIDTH=10 MARGINHEIGHT=10`
`SRC="info.html" name="info">`
❻ `</FRAMESET>`
`</FRAMESET>`
❼ `<NOFRAMES>`
❽ `<BODY> If you had frames, you'd be home`
`by now.`
`</BODY>`
❾ `</NOFRAMES>`
`</HTML>`

❶ **<FRAMESET>** defines the parameters of the frames. This document has two nested framesets. The first defines two rows. Rows are the horizontal areas, one on top of the other. The top will be for the header, and the bottom row will have another **<FRAMESET>** with two columns.

The first row is 108 pixels high. Netscape uses 8 of those pixels for the frame itself, and the graphic is 100 pixels high. Frame sizes can also be defined in terms of percentages (25%) instead of pixels. When you are using a graphic with a known size, it is more useful to define the size of the frame in terms of pixels.

The second row is defined with an *, which lets the browser use the rest of the space at its own discretion. It will take up whatever space is left after the 100 pixels of the first row are allocated.

❷ The **<FRAME>** tag is used to specify the contents of an individual frame. The **SRC=** attribute specifies header.html as the initial content of the frame; **MARGINWIDTH** and **MARGINHEIGHT** declare the margin sizes (zero in this case, to put an image right up to the borders); **NORESIZE** tells the browser to disallow resizing by the user; **SCROLLING="no"** gets rid of any scrollbars; and **NAME="header"** names the frame for use by **<TARGET>** tags later on.

③ The second row has another **<FRAMESET>** tag instead of a **<FRAME>** tag. This is for splitting the row. Two columns are defined: the first column will take up 200 pixels on the left side of the row, and the second column will take the remaining lateral space in the row.

④ Each **<FRAME>** tag defines the next undefined frame specified in the immediately preceding **<FRAMESET>** tag. This one is for the first column from the **<FRAMESET>** in #3 . . .

⑤ . . . and this one is for the second column from the **<FRAMESET>** in #3,

⑥ The **<FRAMESET>** tag requires an ending **</FRAMESET>** tag to tell the browser that it is done defining.

⑦ Everything between **<NOFRAMES>** and **</NOFRAMES>** will be ignored by a frames-capable browser. The content within this section is what will be seen by people whose browsers cannot render frames.

⑧ The **<BODY>** tag is required in the **<NOFRAMES>** section. You can use it as you would in a normal HTML document.

⑨ This ends the **<NOFRAMES>** section.

header.html • This document is nested within the top frame of framed.html.

```
<HTML>
<HEAD><TITLE>Hey! I thought I was in
a frame!</TITLE></HEAD>
<BODY BGCOLOR=33cccc>
<IMG SRC="title.gif" WIDTH=600 HEIGHT=100>
</BODY>
</HTML>
```

① Because each HTML document could end up on someone's screen outside of a frame, it's a good idea to give it a **title** anyway.

② When you give a framed document a **background color**, the background of the frame takes on the color. This document has a background color that is the same as the background of the title graphic. That way, if someone's screen is bigger than our graphic, it blends seamlessly.

③ The body of the document is just the **image**.

165

menu.html • This document is nested within the left frame of framed.html.

info.html • This document is nested within the right frame of framed.html.

```
<HTML>
<HEAD>
❶ <BASE TARGET=info>
<TITLE>Huh? I thought I was in a
frame!</TITLE>
</HEAD>
<BODY BGCOLOR=000066 TEXT=00ccff
LINK=00ffcc VLINK=00ffcc ALINK=00ccff>
<H2>Menu</H2>
❷ <MENU>
    <LI><A HREF=info.html>Info</A>
    <LI><A HREF=milk.html>Milk</A>
    <LI><A HREF=blue.html>Blue</A>
    <LI><A HREF=light.html>Light</A>
    <LI><A HREF=monster.html>Monsters!</A>
</MENU>
</BODY>
</HTML>
```

❶ The **<BASE>** tag has a **TARGET** attribute so that all the hyperlinks load in the frame named "info."

❷ The **<MENU>** tag is used to create a menu in the left-hand frame. Be sure to keep all your menu text as short as possible so that it fits in the frame.

Alternatively, you could create a vertical imagemap designed to fit precisely in the frame.

```
<HTML>
<HEAD>
❶ <TITLE>Info!</TITLE></HEAD>
<BODY BGCOLOR=cccc99>
❷ <H2>Info</H2>
<P>Frames can be a useful tool, when used
carefully.
</BODY>
</HTML>
```

Each of the documents in the right-hand frame is structured as a normal HTML document. It's important to keep the amount of text to a minimum so that it fits nicely in the limited space of the frame.

❶ The **<TITLE>** tag describes the document, for people who might load it outside of a frame.

❷ All the HTML in the document is designed just as you would in a document that was not going in a frame.

extra frame-related HTML attributes

There are a few other frame-related tags that have not been reviewed here.

✎ **Scrolling:** If the image inside a frame is bigger than the browser window, a scrollbar automatically appears. If you want to turn off that scrollbar, you could add this code:

```
SCROLLING=NO
```

✎ **Target:** When you set up client-side imagemaps, you can set a TARGET attribute to instruct the link to target another browser window besides this one it's in. Here's a list of TARGET attributes.

```
TARGET="_self" is the default way frames
work, even without this tag. It means that
the linked reference will appear inside the
same frame that is already visible.

TARGET="_blank" will open a new browser win-
dow, while leaving the old one behind it.

TARGET="_top" takes you to the referenced URL
without keeping it inside your frameset.

TARGET="_parent" removes all the frames on
your page and shows you the referenced link
in its own window.
```

✎ **Borders Off:** Frame borders can be annoying—just like blue borders around images. They call attention to shapes of the defined regions, rather than enabling irregularly shaped graphics to appear seamless. You can turn off borders of frames by using the BORDER=0 tag. Here's an example.

```
<FRAMESET COL=*,120" FRAMEBORDER="no" FRAME-
SPACING="0" BORDER="0">
```

✎ **Border Color:** You can additionally match a border color to your background color, to further eliminate the edges of the border. This would be done like this.

```
<FRAMESET COL=*,120" FRAMEBORDER="no" FRAME-
SPACING="0" BORDER="0" BORDERCOLOR="FFFFFF">
```

summary

One of the coolest things about the web is that you can link viewers anywhere you want on your site. With that freedom comes some new responsibilities, such as how to structure the navigation visually and technically. Here is a summary of this chapter's main points:

✎ Borders around graphics signify that they are clickable. If you take the borders off, make sure that your image invites users to click on a link. The telltale hand icon will appear as their mouse travels over your artwork.

✎ Navigation bars are extremely important on your site. Make sure they appear on every page, in case someone enters your site from a bookmark.

✎ Using rollover techniques is one way to get around using predictable 3D button graphics for linked images. This chapter offers many suggestions for visuals that infer clickability.

✎ If you are going to use server-side imagemaps, you'll have to ask your Internet Service Provider what type of server they use—NCSA or CERN—before beginning work on the map definition file.

✎ Frames offer the ability to leave part of a page stationary, while other parts can change. This is excellent for navigation bars, but don't go too crazy with frames. They can be extremely annoying to your audience, especially if they require that data within framed regions be scrolled in order to be viewed.

horizontal rules

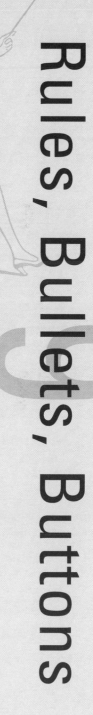

Web graphics have coined a few graphic conventions of their own, such as horizontal rules, bullets, and buttons. This chapter examines the reasons behind these conventions, and the techniques and tools required to implement them.

A horizontal rule that serves as a page divider is something you'll rarely see in print design. These divider lines are commonly observed across web sites the world over, however. Some are embossed, some are thick, some are thin, and some are colored or have different shapes. The web term for these lines is horizontal rule, and they are used for defining a page break, completing an idea, beginning a list, or separating one picture from another.

Horizontal rules are used often; some might even say too often. That's no wonder, if you ask me. Web pages have no set length like printed pages. The visual techniques and metaphors available to print designers—such as using a block of color behind text or images, changing the text color in an isolated paragraph or sidebar, or using a different screened-back image or picture frame to separate an idea or theme—are not easily replicated on the web.

If you want to add horizontal rules to your pages, you have some choices. You can use HTML code, or you can insert your own artwork to make custom horizontal rules and vertical rules, too. When all else fails, there are also libraries of horizontal rule clip art found all over the web. A list of clip art is provided at the end of this chapter.

169

horizontal rules, the HTML way

The basic HTML standard horizontal rule tag looks like this: <HR>. Here it is in the context of code.

```
<HTML>
<BODY>
Some Text
<HR>
Some More Text
</BODY>
</HTML>
```

> Some Text
> ─────────────
> Some More Text

The <HR> tag will put an embossed, double-pixel line horizontally through your page at whatever point you insert it into an HTML document. If you stretch your browser window wider, the horizontal rule will get wider, and vice versa if you narrow your window. Horizontal rules have no set width, except to fill the horizontal distance of your browser screen.

Sometimes you might want to add some breathing room because the horizontal rule will butt up underneath whatever text or image that was in the HTML code before it. The following code adds a row of empty space above and beneath the rule.

```
<HTML>
<BODY>
Some Text
<P>
<HR>
<P>
Some More Text
</BODY>
</HTML>
```

> Some Text
>
> ─────────────
>
> Some More Text

If you want to add more breathing room between your text and rules, insert a paragraph break with the <P> tag.

fancier horizontal rule tags

An advanced course in horizontal rule-making includes:

- Changing the rule's width

- Changing the rule's weight (thickness)

- Changing both the rule's width and weight

- Aligning the rule

- Eliminating fake emboss shading

Notice that if you define a width, the resulting horizontal rule is automatically centered. Any value you put after the = (equal) sign tells the rule how wide to be in pixels.

Here's the code telling the rule to be 10 pixels wide.

```
<HR WIDTH=10>
```

Using a WIDTH attribute adjusts the length of the line.

The following code changes the weight, or thickness, of the line. Notice this stretches the length of a page.

```
<HR SIZE=10>
```

By changing the SIZE attribute, the entire line gets thicker.

The following code changes the thickness and width at the same time. Here's an example that shows the results of code specifying the rule to be a square—equal height and width.

```
<HR SIZE=25 WIDTH=25>
```

By setting the size and width to the same value, you can create rectilinear shapes such as this square.

The following aligns the square left and sizes it at 10 pixels high and 10 pixels wide.

```
<HR ALIGN=left SIZE=10 WIDTH=10>
```

You can use alignment tags on horizontal rules, too.

Look, no fake emboss shading!

```
<HR NOSHADE>
```

The NOSHADE attribute creates a black line.

do-it-yourself horizontal rules

Anything gets old when you see it too often, and horizontal rules are no exception. If you want to be a little more creative, here are some tips to creating custom artwork to design your own rules. When you create your own horizontal rule art, your artwork dictates the length, width, and height. It's a graphic like any other graphic. It can be aliased, anti-aliased, a GIF, a JPEG, interlaced, transparent, blurred, 2D, 3D—you name it. If you know how to make it, it can be a horizontal rule.

To include a graphic as a horizontal rule, the HTML code would be:

```
<IMG SRC="your_horizontal_rule_art_here.gif">
```

clip art rules, too

There are many kind, generous souls on the web who lend their wares for free, as well as other gifted souls who may charge for their art so that they can do what they're good at—satisfy you and me—and still feed themselves and their families. Clip art is a wondrous thing in a pinch, and with tools such as Photoshop, Illustrator, and Painter, there's no end to the cool ways you can personalize clip art files. Make sure that the images are royalty free in the respective licensing agreements if you are going to modify them. Some authors have stipulations that must be honored. Read the readmes!

Here are some clip art collections that I think are cool:

- **Gifs R Us**—Jay Boersma's prolific image collection:
  http://www.ecn.bgu.edu/users/gas52r0/Jay/home.html

- **Sandra's Clip Art Server**—an excellent resource for clip art over the Net:
  http://www.cs.yale.edu/homes/sjl/clipart.html

- **Buttons, Cubes, and Bars**—a great collection of custom art from Chris Stephens:
  http://www.cbil.vcu.edu.8080/gifs/bullet.html

- **Yahoo search for Clip Art**—a sure bet to find the best and latest clip art listings:
  http://www.yahoo.com/Computers_and_Internet/Multimedia/ Pictures/Clip_Art/

bullets

You'll see plenty of pages with diverse information content on the web, but lists of one type or another are universally needed on the majority of sites. List items can appear indented with numbers or preceded by icons known as bullets. Bullets on the web can look standardized, using solid circles in front of text (much like those generated by a word processor), or they can include custom artwork that looks more typical of a CD-ROM or magazine page layout. Creating custom bullets is similar to creating custom horizontal rules. Basically, any artwork that you're capable of creating is a candidate for bullet art.

When designing bulleted lists for the web, you can choose from either HTML bullets or image-based bullets. HTML bullets are created by using code tags that identify the type of list you are creating; such bullets appear as basic circles or squares. Image-based bullets are those you generate from clip art or your own artwork, and they can be used to enhance a list or provide added functionality, such as links. This next section shows you how to create both HTML and image-based bullets, including several variations on both themes.

creating HTML bulleted lists

Using HTML-based bullets is certainly less work than creating your own custom artwork. Sometimes, they're more appropriate, as well. Simple and clean design often looks best without a lot of custom artwork on a page. There will be many instances where an HTML-based bullet or indent will do the job more effectively than custom bullet artwork.

To create a list with solid circle bullets, use the <UL> tag, which stands for unorganized list. To create such a bulleted list within text items, use the <UL> tag along with the <LI> (list item) tag, as shown in the following code.

```
<P>
<UL>
<LI> The first thinga-dingy
<LI> The second thinga-dingy
<LI> The third thinga-dingy
</UL>
```

Using the "unordered" list tags , and "list item" tags produces this result:

- The first thinga-dingy
- The second thinga-dingy
- The third thinga-dingy

The results of using the <UL> tag.

Lists can be nested by inserting a new tag where you want the list to indent or move to another level. The following code uses an additional <UL> tag to create a bulleted list nested within another bulleted list.

```
<P>
<UL>
<LI> The first thinga-dingy
<LI> The second thinga-dingy
<LI> The third thinga-dingy
```

```
<UL>
<LI> More types of thinga-dingies
<LI> Yet More types of thinga-dingies
<LI> Even more types of thinga-dingies
</UL>
```

You can nest lists within lists, by repeating the "ordered" or "unordered" list tags. The results look like this:

- The first thinga-dingy
- The second thinga-dingy
- The third thinga-dingy
  - More types of thinga-dingies
  - Yet More types of thinga-dingies
  - Even more types of thinga-dingies

You can nest bulleted points by adding multiple <UL> tags before the close </UL> tag.

You can have the items in your list be links to other pages or sites by using the <A HREF></A> tag within an organized list or an unorganized list. The following code shows how to use link tags to include links within a bulleted list.

```
<P>
<UL>
<LI> <A HREF="http://www.domain.com">
The first thinga-dingy</A>
<LI> <A HREF="http://www.domain.com">
The second thinga-dingy</A>
<LI> <A HREF="http://www.domain.com">
The third thinga-dingy</A>
</UL>
```

Including links within a list is a matter of using link tags within lists. The results look like this:

- The first thinga-dingy
- The second thinga-dingy
- The third thinga-dingy

The items in your list can be straight text or linked text, just by changing a few tags.

creating ordered and definition lists

At times, you may not want your lists to be preceded with bullets. When creating a list of steps to be followed in order, for example, using numbers rather than bullets will help get your point across. Such numbered lists are called ordered lists. Likewise, lists such as glossaries can appear with indents rather than bullets or numbers. These lists are known as definition lists.

To make a list that automatically generates numbers in front of its items, use the <OL> (ordered list) tag. The following code lines show how to use the <OL> tag to produce a numbered list.

```
<P>
<OL>
<LI> The first thinga-dingy
<LI> The second thinga-dingy
<LI> The third thinga-dingy
</OL>
<P>
```

Using the "ordered list" would automatically generate numbers, instead of bullets in front of each "list item":

1. The first thinga-dingy
2. The second thinga-dingy
3. The third thinga-dingy

The <OL> tag generates ordered (numbered) lists.

If you want to indent items in a list without seeing a bullet shape, you may want to use a <DL> (definition list) tag instead of creating an organized list or unorganized list. You use the <DT> tag for the flush left items and the <DD> tag for the indented items, as shown in the following code.

```
<DL>
<DT>
Thingy Dingies<P>
<DD>The first thinga-dingy
<DD>The second thinga-dingy
<DD>The second thinga-dingy
</DL>
```

Thingy Dingies

The first thinga-dingy
The second thinga-dingy
The second thinga-dingy

Using the <DL> definition list tags creates indented lists.

If you want to change the shape of the automatically generated bullets, you can use the <TYPE=circle> or <TYPE=square> tags, as shown in the following code.

```
<UL>
<LI TYPE=circle>Circle-shaped Bullet
<LI TYPE=square>Square-shaped Bullet
</UL>
```

● Circle-shaped Bullet
□ Square-shaped Bullet

Using the TYPE attribute can change the shape of HTML bullets.

175

more variations for lists

The following code shows variations of the <TYPE> tag, which produce these results:

```
<OL>
<LI TYPE=1> Thingy One
<LI TYPE=1> Thingy Two
<LI TYPE=1> Thingy Three
<P>
<LI TYPE=A> Thingy One
<LI TYPE=A> Thingy Two
<LI TYPE=A> Thingy Three
<P>
<LI TYPE=a> Thingy One
<LI TYPE=a> Thingy Two
<LI TYPE=a> Thingy Three
<P>
<LI TYPE=I> Thingy One
<LI TYPE=I> Thingy Two
<LI TYPE=I> Thingy Three
<P>
<LI TYPE=i> Thingy One
<LI TYPE=i> Thingy Two
<LI TYPE=i> Thingy Three
```

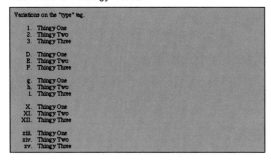

An example of all the different types of HTML-generated bullets .

Alphabetic and Numeric Variety

You can also set up organized lists by using alphabetic and roman numeric criteria with the variations shown in the table below.

lists by alphabet & number

Tag	List Type	Example
<TYPE=1>	Numbers	1, 2, 3
<TYPE=A>	Uppercase letters	A, B, C
<TYPE=a>	Lowercase letters	a, b, c
<TYPE=I>	Uppercase Roman	I, II, III
<TYPE=i>	Lowercase Roman	i, ii, iii

creating custom-made bullets

If you want to use bullets that show more creativity than the basic square or circle, or if you need added linking functionality, you can create your own custom-made bullets. They may be ornamental, where their sole purpose is to decorate the beginning of a list item, or functional, where they serve as linking icons.

If you plan to make your own artwork or use clip art for buttons, you'll need to use different HTML tags to make the art behave as you want. For visual enhancement only, use the <IMG SRC> tag to include image-based bullets at the front of a list, as shown in the following code example. You won't use the <OL> or the <UL> tags because the image itself is what is creating both the bullet and the indent. Note that you do have to put a <BR> tag at the end of each list item to tell the browser to jump to a new line for the next entry in the list. This wasn't necessary when working with the HTML tags because it's a built-in part of the list functionality. I've also used an alignment tag to flow the type properly next to the artwork. Here's the code.

```
<IMG SRC="garrow.gif"
ALIGN=middle> Important Item One<BR>
<IMG SRC="garrow.gif"
ALIGN=middle> Important Item Two<BR>
<IMG SRC="garrow.gif"
ALIGN=middle> Important Item Three<BR>
<IMG SRC="garrow.gif"
ALIGN=middle> Important Item Four<BR>
```

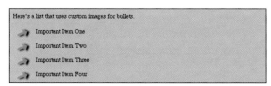

This shows the result of using an <IMG SRC> instead of HTML-generated bullets. The green arrow is a separate piece of art that's been used multiple times on this page.

If you want to use the bullets as icons to link to another site or page, use the <A HREF></A> tag, as shown in the following code example. Because linked images typically have a blue border around them, you'll want to use the BORDER=0 tag inside the <IMG SRC> tag. (Read more about this in Chapter 8, "Links, Maps, Frames.")

```
<P>
<A HREF><IMG SRC="lynda.gif"
ALIGN=middle BORDER=0></A> Lynda<BR>
<A HREF><IMG SRC="jamie.gif"
ALIGN=middle BORDER=0></A> Jamie<BR>
<A HREF><IMG SRC="stinky.gif"
ALIGN=middle BORDER=0></A>Stinky<BR>
<A HREF><IMG SRC="elmers.gif" ALIGN=middle
BORDER=0></A> Elmers<BR>
<A HREF><IMG SRC="jasonjr.gif"
ALIGN=middle BORDER=0></A> Jason Jr.<BR>
<A HREF><IMG SRC="climber.gif"
ALIGN=middle BORDER=0></A>Climber<BR>
<A HREF><IMG SRC="sam.gif"
ALIGN=middle BORDER=0></A>Sam (whose tail
is growing back)
<BR>
```

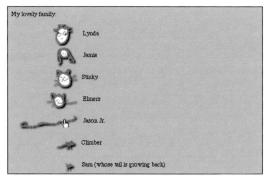

This example shows using the <IMG SRC> tag again, but the artwork inside each tag has been changed.

177

creating custom bullet art

Any paint program provides a good experimentation ground for making custom bullet artwork. There are no specific guidelines except to keep in mind the scale of the type the bullets will precede. It's very difficult to design anything with much detail that is small enough to match the scale of 12-point type, such as those typically generated by HTML. If you want to make larger icons for custom bullets, be sure to enlarge the type in the list as well. More info on controlling type size is available in Chapter 10, "Typography." Here are some tips I can share from my bullet-making explorations, but please don't let them limit your imagination.

step-by-step

Using Kai's Power Tools

KPT filters, which are available for Mac and PC versions of Photoshop, have a nifty plug-in called KPT Glass Lens. If you are looking to create a shiny, 3D bubble button, this simple filter does it automatically for you. Just perform the following steps:

☞ 1   Open a new Photoshop file and fill the background with whatever color it is going to be.

☞ 2   Use the circular Marquee tool to select a small circle. (You can choose to anti-alias, depending on whether you'll use transparency or not. See Chapter 6, "Transparency," for more information on transparency and anti-aliasing.)

☞ 3   Fill the shape with your background color or whatever color you'd like your button to be.

☞ 4   Go to the Filters menu and choose Distort, KPT Lens Glass Bright. A dimensional bubble button will magically appear.

☞ 5   Use the rectangular marquee when finished and make a tight selection around the bounding shape of the bubble. Choose Crop, located under the Edit menu. This makes the file the appropriate size, and it's ready to save. If you want to create an indent in front of or after the custom art, make the shape of the selection account for it before you crop. Follow the rules of Chapters 6, "Transparency," for saving the artwork.

☞ 6   Whether the artwork is meant to have a transparent background, go over a pattern background, or incorporate the solid background dictates whether to save in GIF87a, GIF89a, or JPEG file format.

The Photoshop file generated using the KPT Glass Lens filter.

This screen uses the gray KPT-generated bullets.

In this example, I made purple buttons instead of gray ones.

button clip art

You'll find clip art for buttons all over the World Wide Web. Clip art buttons follow the same rules for custom bullet art; use the <IMG SRC> tag if you want the button for decoration only and the <A HREF=BORDER=0></A> tag if you want them to link. Clip art typically already exists in web file formats GIF or JPEG, and if not, you can use Photoshop to convert them.

Bullets can be abstract, such as dots and cubes, or an icon that actually means something. Michael Herrick, of www.matterform.com, has invented something called QBullets, after "cue-bullet," or bullets that cue you to their hint or function. These buttons are part of a proposed interface standard that his site discusses in detail.

Basically, the idea is that QBullets let your audience know what the subject of your list is by using visual metaphors. The e-mail button is a miniature envelope, the download button looks like a floppy disk, a new item has the word "new item," and so on. Herrick's opinion is that bullets should inform your reader about what is at the other end of the link—large download, outside web site, ftp, telnet, form, and so on.

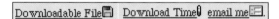

A close-up view of some of the QBullets Herrick has created.

Here's a sample image that shows the Legend page from Herrick's site. QBullets can be used free of charge in exchange for a credit and a link to his page: ✉ http/www.matterform.com.

summary

Working with rules, bullets, and buttons on the web is a lot less straight-forward than in a text or print document. It requires a mixture of programming and design skills. The contents of this chapter are summarized here:

- Horizontal rules, bullets, and buttons can be added by using either HTML or custom graphics. Graphics will take longer to download, but they can add a lot more originality to a page design.

- It's helpful if you make your buttons and bullets mean something rather than just exist for decoration. You may want to refer to Michael Herrick's Matterform page at http://www.matter-form.com.

web-based type

There is a fundamental controversy associated with web design. You have your HTML purists and programmers, and you have your design purists and non-programmers, and often they do not agree or find common ground. Visual design is about control. Typography is an incredibly powerful visual design medium, but good typography requires much more control than HTML currently affords. HTML is about display flexibility and cross-platform distribution of information. HTML and browser support of specific tags are the vehicles with which web pages are delivered, and design is the vehicle with which they are delivered artistically.

This chapter was written to help each side of the design and programming fence understand the other. It will help designers learn tricks to make web typography look as good as it can and will help programmers understand what designers want from HTML.

This chapter covers the following topics:

✎   HTML type

✎   Type alignment tricks

✎   Font usage in HTML pages

✎   Images as type

✎   Anti-aliased type versus aliased type

Typography

10

HTML type versus graphical

There are basically two kinds of typographical elements on the web (or the printed page, for that matter): body type and headline type. Body type, often referred to as body copy, composes the bulk of the written text. Body type is typically smaller and contains the majority of the written content of a web page. Headline type is typically larger and is used to quickly draw the viewer's eye to it, help define a page break, or organize multiple ideas.

You can make body and headline type a couple of different ways on the web. One way involves using HTML and specialized font tags.

The alternative way is to create graphics that have images of type as the visual content instead of pictures. This kind of image-based type is referred to in this chapter as graphic-based type. HTML type is ideal for body copy and graphic-based type is ideal for headlines. This chapter examines procedures for using standard HTML type, adding specialized type tags, and methods for making graphic images with headline type using Photoshop and Illustrator. Understanding some of the aesthetic issues related to type design principles is important before we move toward specific production methods.

aesthetic considerations

I think the web is an incredibly great way to gather information. Typically, when I find a page with a lot of text on it though, I'll print the page on my printer rather than sit and read through the text on my screen. Who wants to have the light of the monitor blaring in their face while having a recreational read? Give me crisp type on paper any day over that! I feel the same way about all computer-based text delivery systems, such as CD-ROMS and interactive kiosks. If you want me to read a lot of text, I'd rather do so on paper. As designers, we have to recognize that computer-based presentations pose distinct challenges and not treat our type-ridden web pages the same way as we would print.

So what design principles can you follow to help out your computer-screen-based reader? I advocate breaking up type into small paragraphs. Also, use different weights, such as bold and italics, to make it possible to skim the page easily and catch the important points. Adding hypertext whenever possible (text that links you from one spot to another, which is typically underlined or bold depending on the way the viewer's browser preferences are set) is another way to break up screen text into more digestible portions. The idea is to break up blocks of text as much as possible. Assume your readers are skimming, and make it easy for them to do.

Understand that you're asking a lot of your end viewer to sit and read pages and pages of type on a screen. It's your job to invent ways to hold his interest and to bring out the important ideas. This is possible through using both HTML and graphic-based text.

typography-based URLs

For the most amazing type glossary to be found on the web, visit
Razorfish's typoGRAPHIC site. This amazing site also teaches about the
principles of type using hypertext at its best. Oh, and a little Shockwave,
Java, and animated GIF action, too!

✍   http://www.razorfish.com/bluedot/typo/glossary/

✍   http://www.razorfish.com/bluedot/typo/

Typofile is an online magazine devoted to type techniques and technology. This site has lots of great tutorials and essays about typography.

✍   http://www.will-harris.com/type.htm

Paul Baker Typographic, Inc. provides a short presentation on basic
typography that includes the use of letter and word spacing, measure,
leading, choosing a typeface, and so on.

✍   http://www.pbtweb.com/typostyl/typostyl.htm

LettError is a two-person virtual design studio. Acclaimed type designers
Just van Rossum and Erik van Blokland work from their respective
homes in The Hague, The Netherlands. Their goal is to create typefaces
that do more than the usual fonts—they create animations, music, typography, web sites, and some graphic design as well. Check 'em out! Be
sure to read their rant on embedded fonts in PDF documents.

✍   http://www.letterror.com/LTR_About.html

Type designer **Thomas Mueller's Liquid Typography** includes his portfolio
and thesis project.

✍   http://www.razorfish.com/thomas/

HTML-based typography

The advantages of using HTML for most body type needs are obvious. First of all, the memory and download time required for using native text is much lower than that used for graphics. Many sites are text-intensive, and using HTML-based type is the only choice to present large quantities of written information in a timely and efficient manner.

The following examples and code demonstrate how to use HTML type tags.

Headings

Headings are created using the <H></H> tag. The heading tags always have to be in the <HEAD> part of an HTML file. Here's some sample heading code.

```
<HTML><HEAD>
<H3>Welcome to this Site!</H3>
<H4>Welcome to this Site!</H4>
<H5>Welcome to this Site!</H5>
</HEAD>
</HTML>
```

Welcome to this Site!

Welcome to this Site!

Welcome to this Site!

Bold

Here are a couple of ways to make type bold.

```
<HTML>
Talk <B>LOUD!</B><P>
Talk <STRONG>LOUD!</STRONG>
</HTML>
```

Talk **LOUD!**

Talk **LOUD!**

Italics

Here are a couple of ways to italicize type.

```
<HTML>
<I> Are you <I>ever going to shut up? </I>
<P>
<EM> Are you <EM> ever going to shut up?
</EM>
</HTML>
```

Are you *ever going to shut up?*

Are you *ever going to shut up?*

Preformatted

Preformatted text usually shows up in Courier or monotype. Here's the code.

```
<HTML>
<PRE> When are you    g   o   i   n   g
to be QUIET?</PRE>
</HTML>
```

When are you   g   o   i   n   g   to be QUIET?

Blinking Text

Caution! Many end viewers find this tag annoying.

```
<BLINK> flash news! </BLINK>
```

Changing Font Sizes

Font sizes can be changed by using the <FONT SIZE>
</FONT> tag. Here's how.

```
<HTML>
Do you ever <FONT SIZE=5>listen</FONT>
to direction anymore?
</HTML>
```

Do you ever **listen** to direction anymore?

Drop Cap

Here's the code for creating drop caps.

```
<HTML>
<FONT SIZE=4>D</FONT>ROP
<FONT SIZE=4>C</FONT>AP
</HTML>
```

DROP CAP

Small Cap

Use the following whenever you want small caps.

```
<HTML>
<FONT SIZE=1>SMALL CAPS </FONT><BR>
</HTML>
```

SMALL CAPS
REGULAR CAPS

Centering Text

Text can be centered by using the <CENTER> tag. Use
the following code.

```
<HTML>
<CENTER>
I'm in the middle...
</CENTER>
</HTML>
```

I'm in the middle...

Useful URLs

Netscape has a site that has a style sheet for
using the <FONT SIZE> tag as well: ✍ http://
www.cen.uiuc.edu/~ejk/fontsizes.html.
Logging on to this site automatically generates an entire range of font sizes by using the
font your browser is set to. In addition, here
are two helpful style sheets that Yoshinobo
Takahas, from Disney Online, shares.

fun with ASCII!

ASCII text was a computer art craze in the 1970s, before computer graphics were something individuals could do easily on personal computers. There were no imaging programs that let people work with vector or bitmap artwork like today, so people made artwork with text characters. Many web pages keep the tradition of ASCII art alive. ASCII art can provide a welcome diversion from typical web art fare.

Publishing ASCII art over the web is a brilliant idea. It has all the advantages of speedy HTML-based text delivery and the advantage of working on almost every browser because the only HTML necessary to produce it involves the <PRE> tag, which is widely supported.

Case Study: Hollywood Records

The Hollywood Records site (✍ http://www.holly-woodrec.com) uses ASCII art for the low-fi (low-bandwidth) version of its site.

Here's a screen-shot of one of its pages that uses ASCII.

Here is the HTML source code for this image.

```
<HTML>
<HEAD>
<TITLE>GWEN MARS Press</TITLE>
</HEAD>
<BODY TEXT="#A99A05" LINK="#A99A05"
VLINK="#FFFFFF" BGCOLOR="#001000">
<CENTER>
<PRE>
<FONT SIZE=+0>
<B>
<A HREF="/HollywoodRecords/Bands/GwenMars/
Press/ Gwen MarsPressM.html">HI-FI GRAFX</A> /
<A HREF="/HollywoodRecords/Bands/GwenMars/
GwenMarsV.html">SCI-FI VR</A> /
<A HREF="/Note">EMAIL US</A> /
<A HREF="/Help">HELP</A>
<A HREF="/HollywoodRecords/HollywoodRecordsL.
html">HOLLYWOOD RECORDS</A> /
<A HREF="/HollywoodRecords/Bands/BandRosterL.
html">MUSICIANS</A> /
<HREF="/HollywoodRecords/Bands/GwenMars/GwenMa
rsL.html">GWEN MARS</A>
</B>
</FONT>
</PRE>
```

```
<PRE>
                                    . . u o e e u u .
                        z $ $ $ R # " " ` ` ` " " " # R $ b L                    . u o d W $ W u
                    : $ $ $ "                          ^ " % .        . o $ R # " " ` ` # $ $ $
                  : $ $ F                                    + "              8 $ $
                8 $ F                                                        $ $ P
              $ $ "                                                        d $ $ "
              $ $ ~                                                      d $ $ "
              $ $ F                                                    d $ $ "
            t $ $                                                    d $ $ "
            $ $ F                                              x @ $ P `
          ' $ $ .                                          . @ $ $ "
          9 $ $ .                            . ~        . @ $ $ #
          9 $ $ .                      . e "      . @ $ $ # `
        z $ $ $ $ &                  . o $ "    u @ $ $ #
      . @ $ $ $ " $ $ $ L        . z $ $ "    z $ $ R "
      : $ $ $ #      ? $ $ $    . o $ $ * "  . d $ $ #
    : $ $ $ "          . o $ $ $ #    z $ $ # `
    @ $ $ "        u @ $ $ $ P "  u @ * "                                          :
  : $ $ $ L  . o $ $ $ $ $ "  . d $ $ $ N                                    d
  : $ $ $ $ $ $ $ $ $ R " `    `    ' # $ $ $ k                        x R
  ' * * * * " "                  " $ $ $ $ e u              d $ "
                                  " $ $ $ $ e u          . u @ $ $ "
                                  " * $ $ $ $ $ $ $ $ $ $ $ $ $ $ # "
                                        ` ` `
</PRE>
<FONT SIZE=+2><B><CODE>PRESS INFO</CODE></B></FONT><P>
</PRE>
</FONT>
</CENTER>
</BODY>
</HTML>
```

The Hollywood Records design team worked with a Mac-based program called Gifscii. GIFscii converts GIFs to ASCII. There are a few other products that enable you to work with ASCII artwork. One good choice is Ascii Paint, which enables you to paint with ASCII characters: ✍ http://www.umich.edu/~archive/mac/graphics/graphicsutil/asciipaint.sit.hqx.

HTML font choices

Chances are, the person looking at your web page is using the default settings for whatever browser he or she is viewing the page from. Most browsers default to using a Times Roman font. I've seen sites that include instructions to the viewer to change their default font to some other typeface. I wish them luck! I know very few web navigators who would take the time to change their settings to see an individual page. If you want your HTML type to be something other than Times Roman, don't count on asking your viewer to change his web browser settings as a foolproof method. In fact, I would imagine an extremely low percentage of viewers would actually act on the suggestion. As an alternative, try the <FONT FACE> tag described next.

Font Face Tag

If you want your audience to see your body copy in a font other than the default font settings, there is a new tag to the rescue, developed by Microsoft, called <FONT FACE>. An explanation of this tag is found at ✍ http://www.microsoft.com/truetype/iexplor/iedemo.htm.

The <FONT FACE> tag enables you to specify which font your page will be displayed in. The main caveat is that your end user must have the font you request installed, or the tag will not work.

Microsoft has a free Mac or PC Web Fonts package that you can download from ✍ http://www.microsoft.com/truetype/hottopic.htm.

```
PACK   All of the above fonts are included in one file for Windows [newfonts.exe: 712KB, self extracting
       archive] or Apple Macintosh [newfonts.sit.hqx: 880KB, BinHex].

Arial, Arial Bold, Italic, Bold Italic
Download Arial for Windows [arial.exe: 397KB, self extracting archive] or Apple Macintosh
[Arial.sit.hqx: 348KB, BinHex].

Times New Roman, Times New
Roman Bold, Italic, Bold Italic
Download Times New Roman for Windows [times.exe: 485KB, self extracting archive] or Apple
Macintosh [TimesNewRoman.sit.hqx: 420KB, BinHex].

Courier New, Courier New
Bold, Italic, Bold Italic
Download Courier New for Windows [courier.exe: 457KB, self extracting archive] or Apple
Macintosh [CourierNew.sit.hqx: 408KB, BinHex].
```

The Web Fonts package includes: Arial, Arial Bold, Arial Italic, Arial Bold Italic, Arial Black, Comic Sans MS, Comic Sans MS Bold, Courier New, Courier New Bold, Courier New Italic, Courier New Bold Italic, Impact, Times New Roman, Times New Roman Bold, Times New Roman Italic, and Times New Roman Bold Italic.

Two problems worth mention occur when you add bold tags or header tags to the <FONT FACE> tag. The results might look funky, so here is some sample code to show you how to use the <FONT FACE> tag.

```
<HTML>
<FONT FACE ="helvetica, arial"> TESTING,
</FONT> one, two, three.
</HTML>
```

TESTING, one, two, three.

To add size variation, add the SIZE attribute to the tag.

```
<HTML>
<FONT FACE="helvetica, arial" SIZE=5> TESTING,
</FONT> one, two, three.
</HTML>
```

TESTING, one, two, three.

To change the color, add the COLOR attribute to the tag.

```
<HTML>
<FONT FACE ="helvetica, arial" SIZE=5
COLOR="CC3366"> TESTING, </FONT>
one, two, three.
</HTML>
```

TESTING, one, two, three.

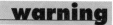

Font Size Differences Between Macs and PCs

No, you are not nuts. If you have a Mac and a PC you will notice that standard 12-point default fonts look different on each platform. Fonts display larger on PCs than on Macs. Sigh. I know you don't want to hear this, but this is one of the cross-platform discrepancy things that there is no real solution for. Except perhaps to serve different pages to Mac and PC end viewers, which is more than a bit too labor-intensive for most site designers. Remember to always check your pages on both platforms and adjust glaring problems.

Here's a screen shot of my site from my Mac.

Here's a screen shot of my site from my PC.

For amusement, I composited the two together in Photoshop using the multiply filter. The size differences with the graphic (the man) are nil, but check out the size differences of the type! Mama mia!

Acknowledge Your Audience

pc	mac
Arial	Helvetica
Courier New	Courier
Times New Roman	Times

The odds are that—even though Microsoft offers the free Web Fonts Package to Mac and PC users—most of your web audience won't even know about it or take the time to install fonts that don't ship on their system. For that reason, it's safest to go with these basic fonts that ship with every Mac and PC.

graphics-based typography

We've just examined many HTML possibilities; now it's time to move on to graphics-based text. Using graphics for text instead of HTML is where you get the chance to flash your type design aesthetic for the world to see. You'll be able to use any font your heart desires and add special effects to it, such as drop shadows, glows, and blurs. A great advantage to using this technique is that the end user will not have to own the font you used or have it installed on his system. Because it's a graphic, it shows up like any other graphic regardless of what system your end viewer uses.

HTML to Place Text Graphics

Placing graphics on a web page is addressed in depth in Chapter 9, "Rules, Bullets, Buttons," and in Chapter 8, "Links, Maps, Frames." The basic way to insert a graphic on a page is to use the <IMG SRC> tag.

Here's how to put the drop shadow artwork, created earlier, on a page.

```
<HTML>
<IMG SRC="dropshad.jpeg">
</HTML>
```

To link the drop shadow image to another source, combine the <IMG SRC> tag with an <A HREF> tag.

```
<HTML>
<A HREF="http://www.domain.com>
<IMG SRC="dropshad.jpeg"></A>
</HTML>
```

This headline was created using text graphics instead of HTML.

Aliasing Versus Anti-Aliasing

Most digital artists prefer the way anti-aliasing looks, but anti-aliasing is not always the best technique when it comes to online legibility. Very small type actually looks worse and quite mushy if it's anti-aliased. Think about HTML type, the type on your computer desktop, and the type in a word processor. Very small type sizes (12 pt. and less) do not look good anti-aliased.

yucky mushy small type that's anti-aliased...

This anti-aliased small type looks bad.

no longer yucky mushy small type because it's aliased

This aliased, HTML type looks much better.

digital foundries

Today there are tens of thousands of PostScript and TrueType fonts available to personal computer users. It's a great benefit to be able to view and order fonts online, especially those late nights when you're designing something that's due the next day and you need a specific font you don't yet own. If you're looking for new fonts, check out these URLs:

- **House Industries:**
  http://www.digitmad.com/house/house.html

- **Letraset Online:**
  http://www.letraset.com/letraset/

- **Handwriting Fonts:**
  http://www.execpc.com/~adw/

- **Fonthead Design:**
  http://www.fonthead.com

- **Fonts Online:**
  http://www.dol.com/fontsOnline/

- **Emigre:**
  www.emigre.com

- **Agfa Type:**
  http://www.agfahome.com/products/
  prodfram/type.html

- **Internet Font Libraries:**
  http://jasper.ora.com:90/comp.fonts/
  Internet-Font-Archive/i ndex.html

Inspirational Typographers

The following individuals are just a few of the many successes, past and present, in type design. You might want to check out literature written by them or about them, as well as research others you find of particular interest. Studying the historical background of typography and learning about 20th-century designers can be a wonderful source of inspiration that effortlessly translates to web-based type design.

- Jan Tschichold

- Laslo Moholy-Nagy

- A.M. Cassandre

- Kurt Schwitters

- Matthew Carter

- David Carson

- El Lissitsky

- Rudy Vanderlands

- Bradbury Thompson

- Lucille Tenazas

- Neville Brody

summary

Typography on the web is challenging because the controls that typographers want are nonexistent in HTML. There are a few good tricks that this chapter covers that will help you break through the limits of HTML:

✎ HTML offers limited control over typography, but even so, it's important to know all the tags and learn to combine them for visually interesting type design.

✎ You can use images of type on web pages, just like images of anything else. This helps break up the predictability of HTML type.

✎ Using the <PRE> tag can help create interesting alignment treatments, as well as allow ASCII art to be embedded in HTML pages.

✎ Visit digital type foundries, and study the masters to get a rich selection of fonts and techniques.

alignment hell

A web page has no fixed size. Some browsers have predefined sizes that the viewing window fits to; others let you size the screen to fill your monitor. Some of your audience will see your page through tiny portable computer screens. Others will have 21-inch monitors. Some of your audience will change the font size defaults, which will make everything line up differently than you planned.

Imagine if you had to fit lots of information on a piece of paper, but no one could tell you the size of the paper you had to work with. And imagine trying to fit that information onto the paper artistically, with a little more finesse than left-justifying every image, headline, and text block. Also imagine that the tools to change position and alignment were strange and unintuitive and didn't work everywhere.

Is it any wonder that few designers know how to do web page layout well? Making a web page behave the way you want it to is a challenging task. This chapter examines alignment issues from several angles:

- Defining the size of a web page

- Using HTML alignment tags

- Using invisible spacers for alignment

- Using tables for alignment

- Aligning foreground and background images

After you've examined all the possibilities this chapter covers, you'll see that it's possible to beat the odds and create interesting layouts in HTML. What is possible is not easy, however, because HTML was never intended to be a page layout description language.

Alignment

193

defining web page size

"Small is better" seems to be the credo of web design. Because there is no fixed size to a web page, you get to define one yourself. Taking into account that people might be looking at your work in small windows, it makes the most sense to define a small page size to work with. Yes, but how small is small?

I tend to err on the conservative side when suggesting width restrictions for graphics on a web page. 640 pixels is the average width of an average computer monitor—even on many portables—and I think there should be some breathing room around that. On the Macintosh, Netscape's opening screen defaults to 505 pixels. I've picked 480 pixels as a good width for an opening graphic or headline. That's the approximate width of the menu bar for Netscape's home page. This rule is not cast in stone. I'm simply describing the sizes of some of the environments your page will be viewed in and arriving at a size based on how I would want my graphics to be viewed.

Lack of a defined web page size can be dealt with creatively. Carina Feldman, who recently received an M.F.A. in graphic design from Art Center College of Design, challenged the unlimited size of a web page by creating a long, vertical text graphic that forces viewers to scroll down many computer screens to finish reading.

Carina Feldman's long, vertical graphic that plays with lack of defined space (✍ www.quicklink.com/~zigzag).

Because web pages can scroll vertically or horizontally, there are no length or width restrictions to contend with on a web document. The size of the artwork you choose to put on any given page dictates the size of the page. If you position artwork that spans horizontally or vertically, the page fits to the size of your artwork. Scroll bars automatically appear in most browsers when the artwork is oversized in either direction.

If you want your opening graphic to be visible on most computer monitors, however, you may want to think about composing your opening page graphic (splash screen or menu bar) so that it can be seen on a portable computer. Most portable computer screens today are 640×480, and some are 640×400.

preparing web graphics

Based on this information, I think opening screen graphics and headline text, or whatever you hope the viewer will see at first glance on your page, should be no taller than 350 pixels.

Some artists choose to make wider screens than my conservative estimate of 480 pixels. There are lots of clever ways to tell your audience how wide to open the browser window, as shown by the following examples.

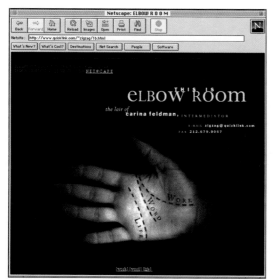

Carina Feldman's site (✍ www.quicklink.com/~zigzag).

The Metatools web site has a page that establishes width and gamma (✍ http://www.metatools.com).

As you can see, the size of your page is up to you. Take your average end viewer's monitor capabilities into account to make informed design decisions about sizing. Carina's pages are great for personal expression, but if you are hired to design a page for a client, it most likely would be important to make the page read at first glance under standard monitor conditions.

Now that the page width and height are understood to be a variables, let's examine techniques for lining up artwork within them.

using HTML for alignment

HTML was not designed to be a QuarkXPress or PageMaker. I don't think the original authors ever dreamed of it as a tool for page layout that would satisfy the needs of graphic designers. It was originally invented to support the scientific community and to include diagrams and image tables that were associated with massive quantities of technical writings. Formatting handles such as left justifying and indenting a list of words suited the needs of that community just fine. We're asking a lot more of HTML than it was ever designed to do, which is OK. HTML originators thought they were inventing one thing for one purpose, and it laid the groundwork for other purposes—including good design!

HTML has limited alignment capabilities, but web designers worth their weight should know how to use all of them. The following section reviews the HTML alignment tags.

Here is a list of HTML tags for aligning text and images.

Text Alignment Tags

These tags relate to text elements. The figure to the right is an example of how they look on a web page.

Paragraph breaks: Insert this tag where you want spaces between paragraphs:

`<P>`

Line breaks: Put this tag where you want to have the text wrap return to the next line:

`<BR>`

Centering text: Use this tag before you center text and/or images and use the closed tag when you want text below it to return to left-justified formatting:

`<CENTER></CENTER>`

Preformatted text: Preformatted text typically uses a different font, such as the typewriter-style Courier, instead of the default Times Roman. The <PRE> tag lets you set the spacing and indents of your type. (For more examples of the <PRE> tag, check out Chapter 10, "Typography.")

`<PRE></PRE>`

No break: Use this tag if you want the browser width to dictate where the text breaks. The closed tag signifies when you want the no-break formatting to end.

`<NOBR></NOBR>`

This shows the preceding tags in action on a web page.

Image and Type Alignment Tags

These tags cause text to align in relationship to the image it's next to.

<ALIGN=TOP> Align text to the top of your image:

```
<IMG SRC="filenamehere.gif" ALIGN=TOP>
```

<ALIGN=BOTTOM> Align text to the bottom:

```
<IMG SRC="filenamehere.gif" ALIGN=BOTTOM>
```

<ALIGN=MIDDLE> Align text to the middle:

```
<IMG SRC="filenamehere.gif" ALIGN=MIDDLE>
```

No Alignment

 "I'm hungry for toast, mama", cried the little piggy

Bottom Alignment

 "I'm hungry for toast, mama", cried the little piggy

Middle Alignment

 "I'm hungry for toast, mama", cried the little piggy

Top Alignment

 "I'm hungry for toast, mama", cried the little piggy

Image Alignment Tags

The following tags align the images to the left or right of the screen.

Image left justified:

```
<IMG SRC="filenamehere.gif" ALIGN=LEFT>
```

Image right justified:

```
<IMG SRC="filenamehere.gif" ALIGN=RIGHT>
```

Right Alignment

"I'm hungry for toast, mama", cried the little piggy

Left Alignment

 "I'm hungry for toast, mama", cried the little piggy

Horizontal and Vertical Space Tags

The horizontal and vertical space tags allow you to insert empty space around a graphic, creating breathing room.

HSPACE: I've used the <HSPACE=XX> tag in the following code to put 40 pixels of breathing room to the left and right of the toaster image.

```
<HTML>
<HEAD> <TITLE> Alignment Test</TITLE> </HEAD>
<BODY BGCOLOR="ffffff">
<IMG SRC="ltoast.jpg" ALIGN=LEFT
HSPACE=40>"I'm hungry for toast, mama!",
<BR>cried the little piggy.<BR CLEAR=all>
</BODY>
</HTML>
```

"I'm hungry for toast, mama!", cried the little piggy.

VSPACE: In order to demonstrate what adding <VSPACE=value> does, I experimented with the following code.

```
<HTML>
<HEAD> <TITLE> Alignment Test</TITLE> </HEAD>
<BODY BGCOLOR="ffffff">
<IMG SRC="ltoast.jpg" ALIGN=LEFT HSPACE=40
VSPACE=80>"I'm hungry for toast, mama!",
<BR>cried the little piggy.<BR CLEAR=all>
</BODY>
</HTML>
```

"I'm hungry for toast, mama!", cried the little piggy.

WIDTH and HEIGHT Attributes

These attributes work by allowing you to specify the width and height values (in pixels) of a graphic. This can accomplish two things: it causes the text on the page to load before the graphic while making space for the graphic to come into the proper location. Using WIDTH and HEIGHT attributes within HTML are very important for downloading speed, and many plug-in <EMBED> tags require that you include width and height information.

There's a lesser-known feature of <WIDTH> and <HEIGHT> tags, however. If you put smaller or larger values in these tags, they will actually shrink or scale your image. In the following example, the actual dimension of the toaster image is 102×115 pixels. By putting a width of 53 and height of 60, I shrunk the image in half. By putting a value of 240×214, I scaled it to be twice as big. The following sections illustrate these alignment tags.

```
<HTML>
<HEAD> <TITLE> Alignment Test</TITLE> </HEAD>
<BODY BGCOLOR="ffffff">
<IMG SRC="ltoast.jpg" WIDTH=53 HEIGHT=60
ALIGN=LEFT>"I'm hungry for toast, mama!",
<BR>cried the little piggy.<BR>
<P>
<P>
<IMG SRC="ltoast.jpg" WIDTH=240 HEIGHT=214
```

```
ALIGN=LEFT>"I'm hungry for toast, mama!",
<BR>cried the little piggy.<BR>
</BODY>
</HTML>
```

This exhausts the possibilities that widely supported HTML tags offer for alignment.

Next, we move on to alignment techniques without HTML. These involve making custom artwork that serves to align images, instead of relying on code.

note

Netscape Proprietary Alignment Tags

Netscape versions 2.0 and above support alignment tags that enable you to create columns and adjust spaces using HTML commands. Since these tags are supported only by Netscape, you run the risk of having to create two sets of pages, or the pages you use these tags on won't display correctly everywhere. For a complete list of these tags, visit:

http://home.netscape.com/eng/mozilla/3.0/relnotes/windows-3.01b1.html#

198

alternatives to HTML

Using images for alignment involves creating spacer art. This art exists on the web page for the sole purpose of making spaces between text and images. For the spacer art to be invisible, you have two options.

Make the spacer art the same color as your background. To do this, use the <BODY BACKGROUND> or <BODY BGCOLOR> tag to create a solid color or colored background pattern tile, or both. These two methods are described in more depth in Chapters 5, "Cross-Platform Color," and 7, "Background Tiles." Here is an example of how this process works.

Or, make sure your spacer art is one color and assign that color to be transparent, saving the one-color artwork as a transparent GIF, as described in Chapter 5, "Cross-Platform Color."

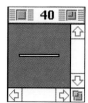

Spacer art.

Using Spacers for Alignment

The following is what the HTML code would produce without using any spacers or alignment techniques. The toaster photographs are from a CD-ROM collection from Classic PIO Partners (800-370-2746). I've named the artwork respectively: ltoast.jpg, ftoast.jpg, and rtoast.jpg.

```
<HTML>
<HEAD> <TITLE> Alignment Test</TITLE> </HEAD>
<BODY BGCOLOR="ffffff">
<IMG SRC="ltoast.jpg">
<IMG SRC="ftoast.jpg">
<IMG SRC="rtoast.jpg">
</BODY>
</HTML>
```

The following is the HTML code to use white spacer art between each image to give them a little breathing room. I made a file in Photoshop that was 40 pixels wide and 1 pixel high, and named it 40space.jpg.

```
<HTML>
<HEAD> <TITLE> Alignment Test</TITLE> </HEAD>
<BODY BGCOLOR="ffffff">
<IMG SRC="40space.jpg">
<IMG SRC="ltoast.jpg">
<IMG SRC="40space.jpg">
<IMG SRC="ftoast.jpg">
<IMG SRC="40space.jpg">
<IMG SRC="rtoast.jpg">
</BODY>
</HTML>
```

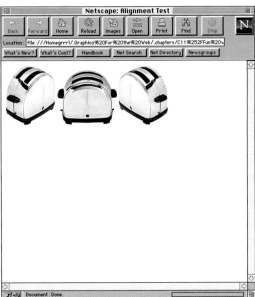

This example uses no spacers.

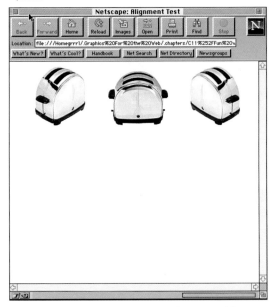

This example uses the 40-pixel wide spacer between each image.

If I used the same spacer in front of each image, I could create a consistent left indent.

```
<HTML>
<HEAD> <TITLE> Alignment Test</TITLE> </HEAD>
<BODY BGCOLOR="ffffff">
<IMG SRC="40space.jpg">
<IMG SRC ="ltoast.jpg">
<P><IMG SRC ="40space.jpg">
<IMG SRC ="ftoast.jpg">
<P><IMG SRC ="40space.jpg">
<IMG SRC ="rtoast.jpg">
</BODY>
</HTML>
```

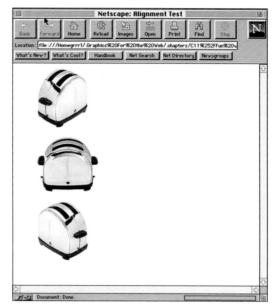

This example uses the space in front of each image.

tip

WIDTH and HEIGHT Attributes for Spacers

You don't have to make the spacer art the correct size. Using the WIDTH and HEIGHT attributes, you can stretch a single-pixel GIF to become any size you wish. David Siegel is the master of the single-pixel GIF trick. Check out his instructions at http:// www.dsiegel.com/tips/wonk5/single.html.

He also wrote a great book, called *Creating Killer Web Sites*, published by Hayden Books (ISBN: 1-56830-289-4), which teaches a lot of wonderful table and alignment techniques.

patterned alignment

One of the frustrating things about web design is the strange offset phenomena that exists between foreground and background images. There's no solution for it, but working with backgrounds that have small intricate patterns, as opposed to large obvious patterns, can trick the eye into forgiving the offset.

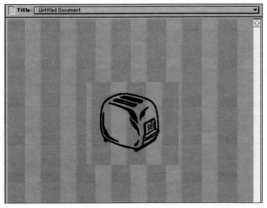

Here's a foreground image that has been precomposited over a complex background in Photoshop.

The identical complex background was used as a seamless tile in the <BODY BACKGROUND> tag of this HTML. Notice the mismatched edge? There's nothing that can be done about this offset, especially because it differs on Mac and PC versions of browsers.

Here's an example by Richard Downs (🖰 http://www.earthlink.net/~downsart/). It's been created against a complex background, but the background pattern is very tight and detailed.

Even though the same offset mismatch exists here, it's barely noticeable because the small pattern is much more forgiving.

202

tables for alignment

Tables for the web were originally conceived to produce columns of text or numbers in individual cells, much like a spreadsheet or chart. Even though tables were invented to support text and numbers, you can put graphics inside table cells, too. All the graphic tags we've described so far work within the table tags. Because of this, I've made a distinction in this chapter between data tables and graphics tables.

You'll see a lot of attention in other books and online sources paid to data tables. The same tags that support data can also support graphics, and herein lies a great power waiting to be unleashed. The graphic designer who knows how to use tables for page layout control will be a much happier camper than the one who doesn't. Learning to program tables will offer lots of formatting options that HTML doesn't directly support.

There are great online tutorials for learning to program tables. I've seen online support only for data tables, not graphics tables. Still, data table principles are crucial to understand if you're going to use graphics tables. Here are my favorite online sources for instruction.

This is a site to watch for all kinds of great online tutorials. The authors are Japanese, so the English is a little stilted, but the instruction on tables and many other HTML tags is absolutely indispensable:

✎   http://ncdesign.kyushuid.ac.jp/howto/text/Normal/table.html

Table instruction from the Netscape site itself:

✎   http://home.mcom.com/assist/net_sites/tables.html

You will learn about how to program graphics tables later in this chapter, but first you should understand the basic kind of web tables: data-based tables.

note

WYSIWYG Tables

It should be noted that almost all WYSIWYG HTML editors let you create tables without programming the code. It's so much easier to use them—instead of coding by hand—that it's really worth your time to invest in one of them. It's important to understand how tables in HTML work, however, because it's still necessary, from time to time, to edit the automatic code WYSIWYG editors generate.

data tables

Data-based tables are probably what the HTML standards committee (✍ http://www.w3c.com) had in mind when they invented the code. These are the typical kinds of tables that you'll see on most sites. They contain text and numbers, links, and occasional graphics. They have telltale borders around the cells, which look slightly dimensional, by employing embossed lines of varying widths to divide individual chart sections.

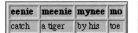 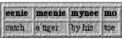

Data tables default to using embossed lines to divide the cells and sections.

If you use a pattern background or solid color background, the embossing shows through and looks as if it's a lighting effect.

Table borders are similar to horizontal rules on steroids—the HTML code magically manufactures vertical and horizontal lines of different widths and thicknesses with a few choice strokes of code and tags. They seem complicated by appearance, but you will probably be surprised at how easy they are to create and use.

HTML Table Tags

When creating data or graphics tables for the web, you work with the same HTML tags. The table tags allow you to put information inside individual cells. Understanding the tag structure for data tables enables you to work with the graphic tables later in this chapter.

You always begin a table with **<TABLE>** and end it with **</TABLE>** tag. The **<TR> </TR>** tag stands for starting and ending a new row. The **<TH> </TH>** tag delineates the header and makes the text in that row bold. The **<TD> </TD>** tag stands for the content of each data cell.

Here's the HTML example of such code:

```
<TABLE>
<TR> <TH>eenie </TH>
<TH>meenie</TH><TH>mynee</TH>
<TH>mo</TH></TR>
<TR><TD>catch</TD><TD>a tiger</TD>
<TD>by his</TD>
<TD>toe</TD></TR></TABLE>
```

eenie	meenie	mynee	mo
catch	a tiger	by his	toe

The **<TABLE BORDER>** tag gives the table that embossed look and feel.

```
<TABLE BORDER>
<TR> <TH>eenie
</TH><TH>meenie</TH><TH>mynee</TH>
<TH>mo</TH></TR>
<TR><TD>catch</TD><TD>a tiger</TD>
<TD>by his</TD><TD>toe</TD></TR></TABLE>
```

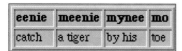

The **<COLSPAN>** tag allows one row to fill more than one column.

```
<TABLE BORDER>
<TR><TH COLSPAN=4> A poem, by someone</TH>
<TR> <TH>eenie
</TH><TH>meenie</TH><TH>mynee</TH>
<TH>mo</TH></TR>
<TR><TD>catch</TD><TD>a tiger</TD><TD>by
his</TD><TD>toe</TD></TR></TABLE>
```

A poem, by someone				
eenie	meenie	mynee	mo
catch	a tiger	by his	toe

The **<ROWSPAN>** tag takes up columns and rows. It is not any specified size or shape; the dimensions are dictated by the content you insert.

```
<TABLE BORDER>
<TR><TH ROWSPAN=4> A poem, by someone</TH>
<TR><TH>eenie
</TH><TH>meenie</TH><TH>mynee</TH>
<TH>mo</TH></TR>
<TR><TD>catch</TD><TD>a tiger</TD><TD>by
his</TD><TD>toe</TD></TR></TABLE>
```

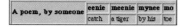

The **<TABLE WIDTH=# of pixels>** and **<TABLE HEIGHT=# of pixels>** tags let you dictate the shape of the table by pixels.

```
<TABLE BORDER WIDTH=300 HEIGHT=100>
<TR> <TH>eenie
</TH><TH>meenie</TH><TH>mynee</TH>
<TH>mo</TH></TR>
<TR><TD>catch</TD><TD>a tiger</TD><TD>by
his</TD><TD>toe</TD></TR></TABLE>
```

The tag **<TABLE CELLSPACING=# of pixels>** puts a thicker line weight around the cells.

```
<TABLE BORDER CELLSPACING=10>
<TR> <TH>eenie
</TH><TH>meenie</TH><TH>mynee</TH>
<TH>mo</TH></TR>
<TR><TD>catch</TD><TD>a tiger</TD>
<TD>by his</TD><TD>toe</TD></TR></TABLE>
```

eenie	meenie	mynee	mo
catch	a tiger	by his	toe

The **<TABLE CELLPADDING=# of pixels>** tag puts a uniform space inside the cells, governed by the number of pixels entered after the = (equal) sign.

```
<TABLE BORDER CELLPADDING=10>
<TR> <TH>eenie
</TH><TH>meenie</TH><TH>mynee</TH>
<TH>mo</TH></TR>
<TR><TD>catch</TD><TD>a tiger</TD>
<TD>by his</TD><TD>toe</TD></TR></TABLE>
```

eenie	meenie	mynee	mo
catch	a tiger	by his	toe

You can adjust the alignment of data inside cells by using the **<VALIGN>** tag, which allows you to specify top, middle, bottom, and baseline alignments.

```
<TABLE BORDER HEIGHT=100>
<TR> <TH>eenie
</TH><TH>meenie</TH><TH>mynee</TH>
<TH>mo</TH></TR>
<TR><TD VALIGN=top>catch</TD>
<TD VALIGN=middle>a tiger</TD>
<TD VALIGN=bottom>by his</TD><TD
VALIGN=baseline>toe</TD></TR></TABLE>
```

eenie	meenie	mynee	mo
catch			toe
	a tiger		
		by his	

You can also specify, right, left, and middle alignment values within the **<TR>**, **<TH>**, and **<TD>** tags by using the word **ALIGN**.

```
<TABLE BORDER WIDTH=300>
<TR> <TH ALIGN=left>eenie </TH>
<TH ALIGN=left>meenie</TH>
<TH ALIGN=left>mynee</TH>
<TH ALIGN=left>mo</TH></TR>
<TR><TD ALIGN=left>catch</TD>
<TD ALIGN=left>a tiger</TD>
<TD ALIGN=left>by his</TD>
<TD ALIGN=left>toe</TD></TR></TABLE>
<TABLE BORDER WIDTH=300>
<TR> <TH ALIGN=right>eenie </TH>
<TH ALIGN=right>meenie</TH>
<TH ALIGN=right>mynee</TH>
<TH ALIGN=right>mo</TH></TR>
<TR><TD ALIGN=right>catch</TD>
```

```
<TD ALIGN=right>a tiger</TD>
<TD ALIGN=right>by his</TD>
<TD ALIGN=right>toe</TD></TR></TABLE>
```

eenie	meenie	mynee	mo
catch	a tiger	by his	toe

You can also put graphics inside tables by using the **<IMG SRC="**name.gif**">** tag, instead of text or values. Here's an example of such code.

```
<TABLE BORDER>
<TR> <TD>
<IMG SRC="catcha.gif"></TD></TR>
</TABLE>
```

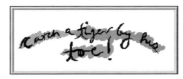

Here's an example of mixing text and graphics inside cells of a table.

```
<TABLE BORDER>
<TR> <TH>eenie </TH><TH>
<IMG SRC="meenie.gif"></TH><TH>mynee</TH>
<TH>mo</TH></TR>
<TR><TD>catch</TD><TD>a tiger</TD>
<TD>by his</TD><TD>
<IMG SRC="toe.gif"></TD></TR></TABLE>
```

eenie	meenie	mynee	mo
catch	a tiger	by his	t oe

This last example shows how to insert graphics into your tables by using the <IMG SRC> tag. The following section explains how you can work with graphics more seamlessly, by eliminating the telltale border around table cells.

without tables

The <PRE> tag, which was discussed in Chapter 10, "Typography," can also be used for alignment purposes. Here's Crystal Water's (author of *Web Concept & Design* and *Universal Web Design* from New Riders) home page. It uses the <PRE> tag exclusively. It's interesting to take a look at Crystal's code.

Check out ✍ **http://www.typo.com for very interesting layout ideas using the <PRE> and <FONT SIZE> tags.**

```
<HTML>
<HEAD>
<TITLE>crystal waters - www.typo.com</TITLE>
</HEAD>
<BODY bgcolor="#000000" text="#cccccc"
link="#cccccc" vlink="#999999">
<code><font size=3>
<A HREF="./about.html"><IMG SRC="./t.gif"
WIDTH="419" HEIGHT="86" vspace="10"
BORDER="0"></A> <A
HREF="./imagedes.html#typologo">D</A>
<br clear=all>
<pre><font size=4 color="#6699FF">crystal
```

```
waters . .     . . . . . . . . . . . .
</font><font size=3>december 1996
<font size=4 color="#6699FF">              .
<A HREF="./new.html">what's
<font size=6>new</font> in typo</A>
<a href="../uwd/uwd.html">the
<font size=6>universal</font> web design
book</a>. . .
                                .
<a href="./lamott/lamott.html">anne lamott
site</a>            . . . . . .
<a href="../technoid/technoid.html">technoid</a>
    . . .    .          .              .

    .            .           .          .

    .              .
<a href="./cool/cool.html">cool connections</a>
         . .   .          .              .
<a href="./writings/writings.html">writings</a>
    .              .
<a href="./pix/pix.html">random pix</a>        .
. . . . . . .  <A HREF="./kudos.html">ego
feed</A>          .              .
. . . . <a href="../crystal/crystal.html">
my biostuff</a>                           .
                                     .

    .
<font size=6>
<A HREF="./store/store.html">book</font>
<font size=5>store</A></font> . . .
<A HREF="./wcd/wcd.html">the
<font size=6>web</font>
<font size=6>concept</font> &
<font size=6>design</font> book</A></pre>
<code><font size=4>
<!--sirius counter II-->
<IMG align=right HEIGHT="32" WIDTH="65"
SRC="/cgi-bin/Count2?uname=crystal¦num=2¦udir=1¦
dtype=num¦dmax=6¦pad=N">
<font size=4 color="#6699FF">. . . . . .
</font><a href="mailto:typo@typo.com">write
typo</a><br clear=all></body>
</html>
```

table-based vertical rules

There are two techniques for creating vertical rules: one using tables and the other using background tiles. Here's how to create a vertical rule using tables:

The first method creates a table using three columns. Where you want the vertical rule to go dictates how you create the columns. I created this example with exact pixel dimensions and percentages.

```
<HTML>
<HEAD>
<TITLE>Vertical Rules!</TITLE>
</HEAD>
<BODY BGCOLOR="#ffffff">
<TABLE WIDTH="441" BORDER="0" CELLSPACING="0"
CELLPADDING="0" HEIGHT="282">
<TR>
<TD WIDTH="28%" VALIGN="TOP" HEIGHT="281">
<P>This enables type to go to the
left of this rule
<P>This enables type to go to the
left of this rule
<P>This enables type to go to the
left of this rule
<P>This enables type to go to the
left of this rule
<P>This enables type to go to the
left of this rule
<P>This enables type to go to the
left of this rule
<P>This enables type to go to the
left of this rule</TD>
<TD WIDTH="7%" VALIGN="TOP">
<IMG SRC="/homegurrrl/pwg/vertical.GIF"
WIDTH="9" HEIGHT="310" ALIGN="TOP">
</TD>
<TD WIDTH="65%" VALIGN="TOP">
<P>This enables type to go in the
right column
<P>This enables type to go in the
right column
```

```
<P>This enables type to go in the
right column
<P>This enables type to go in the
right column
<P>This enables type to go in the
right column
<P>This enables type to go in the
right column
<P>This enables type to go in the
right column
<P>This enables type to go in the
right column
<P>This enables type to go in the
right column</TD></TR>
</TABLE>
</BODY>
</HTML>
```

This enables type to go to the left of this rule	This enables type to go in the right column
This enables type to go to the left of this rule	This enables type to go in the right column
This enables type to go to the left of this rule	This enables type to go in the right column
This enables type to go to the left of this rule	This enables type to go in the right column
This enables type to go to the left of this rule	This enables type to go in the right column
This enables type to go to the left of this rule	This enables type to go in the right column
This enables type to go to the left of this rule	This enables type to go in the right column
This enables type to go to the left of this rule	This enables type to go in the right column
This enables type to go to the left of this rule	This enables type to go in the right column

Here's what the finished table looks like with the vertical rule.

tile-based vertical rules

The second method is much more simple. Create a tiled background image that includes a vertical stripe. Using the <BODY BACKGROUND> tag discussed in depth in Chapter 7, "Background Tiles," you can make this image repeat and look like a long vertical rule.

This is what the source artwork looks like for the repeating tile.

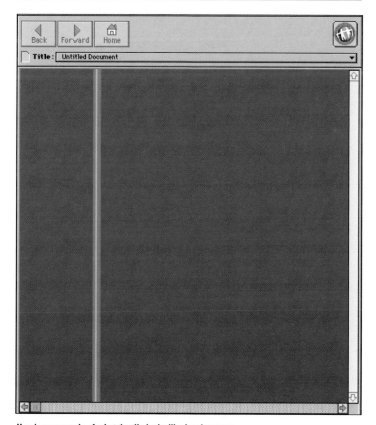

Here's an example of what the tile looks like in a browser.

summary

Creating well aligned web pages is a challenge and an art. This chapter offers suggestions using artwork and HTML, which give you the tools to master alignment techniques.

- There is no fixed size to a web page, but it's important to pay attention to the standard size monitor screen of 640×480 as you design your site.

- It's possible to use a combination of HTML and Netscape-specific tags to create alignment for images and text.

- You can use invisible spacer artwork to nudge alignment into obedience. Using <HEIGHT> and <WIDTH> tags can change the size of the spacers to force artwork in different directions.

- Many page designers use tables to ensure accurate and pleasing alignment.

- Create vertical rules using tables or background tile artwork.

web animation

An unfortunate irony is that animation is a lot easier to enjoy as a passive spectator than it is to create. For many newcomers to web page creation, there's never been a reason to consider learning how to create animation until now. For others, even experienced animators, the web is new territory with different rules, standards, terminology, and tools to understand. The maturing web of today is actually bustling with animation choices—from how to make the content to what tools to use to what delivery methods and file formats to choose from.

The web has introduced many new concepts to us, and adding animation to web pages introduces more. First of all, people used to working in film or video have never had to give much thought to the file size of their artwork. On the web, file size translates to speed. If you don't think speed is important, think about how annoyed you get when pages don't load quickly enough. Animation, by nature, relies on displaying multiple images. Each image takes its own amount of time to download. This poses a major challenge to animation developers and authors that extends beyond the normal complexities of animation creation and delivery in other mediums.

Animation

12

animation decisions

There used to be a much wider disparity between browsers—those that supported certain tags and features over those that didn't. One good thing to say about competition is that the major browsers of today (Netscape and Microsoft Internet Explorer) support plug-ins, Java, GIF Animation, JavaScript, and server push. Lagging seriously behind is AOL and other much lesser-known browsers. Fortunately, AOL is making it possible for its customers to view the web with Microsoft Internet Explorer now, so even that last hurdle of browser inconsistency is disappearing. This is not to say that standards for the web are ironed out or at peace with each other. Change and new standards are the norm on the web, not the exception.

All these factors lead to new decisions for the web designer. Questions such as which technologies to invest in, which new tools to learn, and the aesthetics and appropriateness of animation are new issues to add to the long existing list of design concerns.

Here are some of the things you'll find in this chapter:

- The aesthetics of animation—when and how much to use?

- Animation technologies

- Animation techniques

- Speed considerations

the aesthetics of animation

Before we get into the what, where, how, and why of animation, I'd like to stop a moment and consider the broader issue—the aesthetics of animation. With the exception of multi-media, the web is the first medium to combine animation and body text on a single page. For this reason, it's no wonder that many people struggle to use animation effectively.

Adding animation to a site can be great, but it can also have the reverse effect by appearing gratuitous and/or annoying to your audience. During a recent panel that I moderated, Ben Olander, Creative Director at Organic Online (✎ www.organic.com), commented, "Most animation you see on the web is the equivalent of the <BLINK> tag." I agree with him, but I also see this as a natural outgrowth of artists and developers who are first working with a new tool.

Here are some very general, personal guidelines I would like to share:

✎ In most instances, animation that cycles endlessly will eventually become annoying. This chapter will teach you how to set up loops, or a finite number of repeats.

✎ If you use more than one animation on a single page, the effect may be overwhelming to the end viewer instead of impressive.

✎ Animation calls attention to itself much more than static images on a page. Make sure that the content of your animation is, in fact, something you want the most attention called to on your page. If it isn't, the animation will effectively detract from what you're trying to communicate.

✎ Make sure your animation loads quickly. You'll learn guidelines to achieve fast downloading speeds in this chapter. If you make your audience wait too long for the animation or plug-in to load, they'll move onward before ever seeing it.

web animation technologies

Before getting into any nitty-gritty techniques and products, it's first important to know what choices you have in terms of different technologies. A brief synopsis of different animation delivery choices follows.

Animated GIFs

Animated GIFs, or for the more technically-inclined, GIF89a's, have been in existence since the late 1980s. The great news is that all the major web browsers have recently flocked to support the spec, making it possible to include these types of files in web pages without worry of excluding any potential end viewers.

The GIF89a file format allows for multiple images to be stored inside a single GIF document. When displayed within browser software that recognizes the multiple images, the artwork streams in to the web page in a predetermined sequence, creating a slide-show style animation. The file format supports looping (the capability to repeat multiple images indefinitely) and timing delays between frames of artwork. GIFs also support limited masking, meaning that animations can use the same type of transparency supported by static GIF images.

Animated GIFs require no plug-ins and no programming, and don't even require a live web connection, making them perfect for intranets and testing locally on your machine. Animated GIFs are simple to make,

easy to include in HTML, and effortless for your web-viewing audience to see. They are one of the most elegant solutions to web animation and lack only in that they cannot include interactivity or sound. For an animated logo or button, however, animated GIFs are a pretty smart option.

To include animated GIFs in web pages, you'll use the standard <IMG SRC> tag. A simple example of the code would look like this:

```
<IMG SRC="my_animation.gif">
```

Specific tools with which to create animated GIFs are discussed later in this chapter. Here are some recommended resources for learning how to create and code animated GIFs:

For a good tutorial on animated GIF options, check out Royale Frazier's amazing animated GIF resource at http://member.aol.com/royalef/gifanim.htm.

Another great tutorial exists at Yves Piguet's (author of GIFBuilder) site: http://iawww.epfl.ch/Staff/Yves.Piguet/clip2gif-home/GifBuilder.html.

Plug-Ins

Many enhanced animation options are possible through plug-ins. Plug-ins need to be installed by the end viewer. This requires that your viewers download the plug-in, install it in their browser plug-in folder, and restart their browser. Plug-ins do not exactly support effortless web surfing, and the truth is, many people will choose to click off a page that requires a plug-in rather than endure the bothersome interruption or time-consuming installation process.

Web plug-ins are barely a year old, and many browsers are just beginning to support them for the first time. This means that plug-in support is sometimes unstable and poorly implemented. If you decide to choose an animation format that requires a plug-in, you should keep in mind that your choice to do so probably excludes a portion of your potential audience. You might consider including a link to download the plug-in before the screen appears that requires it. Notifying your audience that you're using a plug-in is a courtesy, and creating alternate pages for those who won't bother with the plug-in installation process is highly recommended.

Typically, whenever you include content that requires a plug-in, you will use an <EMBED> tag within your HTML. You must always put in the <HEIGHT> and <WIDTH> tags to define the size for any plug-in or Java content on a web page. The <NO EMBED> tag will display alternate content. A sample line of code that includes a plug-in-reliant file might look like this:

```
<EMBED="myanimationfile.xxx" HEIGHT="200" WIDTH="200">
<NO EMBED="alternatecontent.gif" HEIGHT="200" WIDTH="200">
```

Java

Java has quickly become one of the most renowned programming languages of our time. People who would have never before considered learning a programming language are clamoring around Java's allure in unprecedented numbers. What's all the hype about, and is Java a good animation delivery medium?

Java's potential benefits are almost as revolutionary as the web itself. Java creates mini-executable-programs (called applets) that promise to be platform-independent, compact enough to travel over phone wires, and able to expand on anyone's system regardless of OS, make, or model. Another great thing about Java is that the popular big three browsers (Netscape, MSIE, and Mosaic) support Java without requiring a plug-in. This, in theory, gives Java high marks for accessibility and compatibility. I know many people who complain that their browsers still choke on Java, so my suspicion is that we'll be waiting a little longer before the hype matches the reality. Regardless, a lot of people and companies are investing heavily in Java, which assures me that the bugs will eventually get ironed out.

Because Java creates custom programs, it has the potential to create computational animation, as opposed to sprite-based animation. In simple English, this means that a Java applet could calculate a changing curve shape on-the-fly, react differently to changeable conditions, or build motion based on external input. Clearly, for the right purposes, Java as an animation delivery medium holds great promise. For simple things, such as moving buttons or animated logos, it's probably overkill. One thing that some Java authors are doing is including plug-ins inside a Java applet so that plug-in content can be viewed effortlessly by spectators who may not have had the proper configuration to begin with. For this reason, Java doesn't have to be mutually exclusive from other animation delivery methods that involve plug-ins or proprietary viewing software.

Java will require an <APPLET> tag to be included in HTML pages. A sample line of code that includes Java-based content might look like this.

```
<APPLET="my_first_java_programming_triumph.xxx"
HEIGHT="200" WIDTH="200">
<NO EMBED="alternatecontent.gif" HEIGHT="200"
WIDTH="200">
```

A good starting point for learning about Java is at Sun's site: ✍ http://java.sun.com/.

QuickTime Movies

There are two ways to include QuickTime on a web page: the old way, which does not require a plug-in, and the new way, which does. The old way was to write QT files into HTML with an <HREF> tag, making sure that the document had a .mov or .qt extension at the end of the file name. This method will cause the file to download. A separate helper application will pop up and play the movie in older browsers, and in newer browsers it will create a new web page with only the QuickTime movie against a gray background.

Here is an example of the HTML for standard QT:

```
<A HREF="PH60709B.mov">
```

The only thing you need to do special to prepare the file is to flatten the QuickTime movie, which changes its resource fork so that platforms other than Macintoshes can play the files. Flattening utilities can be found at ✍ ftp://ftp.utexas.edu/pub/mac-graphics/flattenmoov.hqx. Or if you own Adobe Premiere, you can use Flatten Movie, found under the Export menu. If you choose to use this older method of including QT movies, be aware that your audience will have to wait for the entire movie to download before they can see a frame of your file. It's courteous to include a warning of the file size on the same web page where the movie link is, to warn in advance of long download times.

In newer browsers, QuickTime can be viewed as an inline (inside the browser) element of a web page.

Apple calls this type of QuickTime file a fast-start movie. This means that you can arrive at a web page, see a movie as an image, and click a play button, and the file will start to play with sound! The lack of long download time and need for external MIME players has obvious appeal over the older method.

In order to create fast-start movies, you must change your HTML and change the way you save your QT movie. A simple drag-and-drop utility called Internet Movie Tool, available free from ✍ http://www.quick-time.apple.com/dev/devsw.html, allows you to convert standard QuickTime movies into fast-start QT movies. Implementing fast-start movies also requires a plug-in, which is available from the QuickTime site: ✍ http://quicktime.apple.com. QT 2.5 flattens and reconfigures the movie to work as a streaming fast-start file for you automatically.

Because a plug-in is involved, the <EMBED> tag is used to write the file into your HTML document. There are all kinds of other spiffy controls you can include in your HTML, such as whether to have play buttons appear or not, or include autoplay or looping functions. A full list of support tags is available from ✍ http://quicktime.apple.com/dev/devweb.html. The plug-in is also available from the same site, and the best news is that Netscape 3.0 ships with this plug-in already installed! HTML tags for embedding fast-start QuickTime movies, as well as a wealth of other information, is availabe at the QuickTime site: ✍ http://quicktime.apple.com.

JavaScript

JavaScript actually has nothing to do with full-fledged Java. Initially the Netscape-originated scripting product was slated to be named Live-Script. With the success of Java, Netscape decided to license the Java name from Sun so that its custom scripting language could bear the same name. The similarities between Java and JavaScript end there!

Java needs to be compiled, meaning that the code is written and then goes through a post-processing routine that finalizes the code and completes the programming process. Compiled code is invisible to the end user. Any type of software on your computer is an example of compiled code—from your word processor to your imaging programs to your browser applications.

JavaScript gets compiled on your end user's machine, which means that the raw code sits inside HTML documents. This is a great boon to those interested in learning to write JavaScript because—just like HTML—you can "view the source" of any web page that contains JavaScript and then copy, paste, and personalize to your heart's content. If you plan to do this, however, it is proper netiquette to credit the original author's name of the JavaScript within your pages that have "borrowed" it.

There aren't many practical examples of JavaScript being used for animation. You can program scrolling text at the bottom of a web page, create a rollover effect with a button, or make a clock tell time, but that is about the extent of what's possible so far.

Good JavaScript Resources

✎ For a great site that supplies JavaScript Tips of the Week, try:
  ✍ http://www.gis.net/~carter/therest/index.html

✎ Excellent tutorials:
  ✍ http://www.webconn.com/java/javascript/intro/

Server Push

Server push has become outdated as an animation delivery for the most part. It involves CGI (**C**ommon **G**ateway **I**nterface) scripting, which extends the capability of HTML and is used for all kinds of things the World Wide Web over, including calculating database data from forms or making server-sided imagemaps. CGI requires that you write a script in any number of real programming languages, the most popular of which are Perl, sh, C++, and AppleScript. If you're going to go through the bother of learning a programming language for animation purposes, most would agree Java would be a superior choice because of its flexibility and nonreliance on a server.

Server push sends a request to the web server to send out frames of an animation. This means that an active connection between the web server and web client must be engaged throughout the animation process. This can tie up precious server time and make your site less accessible to large numbers of visitors. The numerous cons (requires programming, taxes the server, and requires live connection to see) outweigh the pros (can supply changing and generate on-the-fly animation content) of this method.

The HTML for server push would link the file to a CGI script. The CGI script would need to be located on the server. The HTML would look something like this.

```
<IMG SRC="push.cgi">
```

tech notes: more on animated GIFs

In my opinion, working with animated GIFs is one of the most sensible choices of web animation formats to choose from. Animated GIFs include the following:

- The capability to set looping, or number of repeats

- The capability to set delays between individual frames

- Download speeds

- The capability to optimize the graphics by using different disposal methods

- Palettes

- Transparency

- Interlacing

Looping: As stated earlier, be careful of unlimited looping animations because they can annoy your audience.

Frame delays: Frame delays can be used to alter the timing of animations. The unit of measurement is 100=1 second. If you want your first frame to last 5 seconds, your next three to last 1 second each, and the last frame to last 15 seconds, your frame delays would look something like this:

```
Frame 01=500
Frame 02=100
Frame 03=100
Frame 04=100
Frame 05=1500
```

Download speeds: The initial download time of the animated GIF will depend on your end user's connection speed, but once the animation has fully downloaded, it will depend on the processor speed of his computer. This can make for wildly different frame delay timings on different systems, regardless of what frame delays you program. Almost all GIF animation software packages support frame delays.

Optimization: Animated GIFs can be optimized, just like regular GIFs. The same rules that applied to file size savings in Chapter 4, "Speedy Web Graphics," apply here. Like other GIFs, you want to make sure that you use as few colors as needed and try to avoid dithering or noise in your image.

Transparency and disposal methods: Disposal methods are a scary sounding term for how the animation is displayed in terms of its transparency. With a single image, this is a nonissue. A transparent image shows through to its background, and that's the end of the story.

With a multiple-frame GIF, however, this presents a bigger issue. Let's say I have an animated ball that's bouncing. If I make the ball transparent, and the image before it has already loaded, the transparency might show part or all of the frame before. Instead of the illusion of motion, the result would be the non-illusion of each frame of my ball bouncing animation visible at once.

The disposal method is what instructs the GIF animation on how to display preceding frames of the animation. Disposal methods are set within whatever GIF animation software package you're using.

Unspecified: Use this disposal method when you aren't using transparency. It will simply present each frame in its entirety and will not yield any added optimization to the file. If I had an animation that changed images every single frame, I would use this disposal method.

Do not dispose: This disposal method would reveal each preceding frame of an animation. Let's say I wanted to create an animation of my name handwriting itself on the screen. If I left the L to draw itself only once and then used the subsequent frame to draw the Y, I would be creating a smaller file size. Use this method when you want the prior frames to show through, and you want to enjoy some file savings with no penalty to image quality.

Restore to background: Instead of displaying the previous frame, the animation is set to show the background color or tile image of your web page.

Restore to previous: This function is almost the same as Do Not Dispose except the first frame always stays visible underneath the rest of the animation. As of writing this book, Netscape did not properly support this function.

Palettes: Most GIF animation software allows you to create bit-depth settings. Lower bit-depth settings will result in smaller, faster animated GIFs. One problem palette management issues in animated GIFs suffer from is that often the software or browser defaults to accepting a different palette for each frame, which will cause palette flashing (a psychedelic feast for the eyes, to be sure)—most likely not the effect you were wishing to see.

The best way to avoid GIF animation palette problems is to map each frame of your animation to a common palette. Instructions for doing this in Photoshop are located in Chapter 5, "Cross-Platform Color."

Interlacing: Interlaced GIFs were discussed in Chapter 3, "Web File Formats." Adding the interlace feature to a single or multiple GIF image will cause it to look blocky until it comes into focus. Personally, I dislike the effect, and especially dislike the effect in the context of animation. It sort of breaks the illusion of motion to see each individual frame come into full focus, don't you think?

For more information on animated GIFs, check out the online resources listed in the "Web Animation Technologies" section of this chapter. If you'd prefer to learn from a book, Richard Koman has written a short and sweet full-color title about GIF animation, with examples on a CD that should help anyone wanting to delve further into the GIF animation creation process:

GIF Animation Studio
Full Color book w/CD
Author: Richard Koman
Imprint: O' Reilley
ISBN: 1-56592-230-1
Price: $39.95 U.S.

creating animation content

There are lots of different animation tools and technologies, but what about the animation content itself? If you've never made animation before, you might be asking what exactly constitutes animation, per se?

Animation is actually the illusion of motion. It's really composed of a series of still images, shown in quick succession—the process of which tricks our minds into thinking that stationary artwork is truly moving. It's all fake! Making artwork for animation is an exercise in understanding how to fake motion through presenting changing artwork over time.

There are all kinds of ways to generate animation files or sequential images that change in appearance from frame to frame. Any number of animation software packages can generate sequential images in PICT, PIC, GIF, or QuickTime formats. Most of the web animation tools can import standard PICT, GIF, or QT formats.

You can make animation without a dedicated animation program, too. If you use an image editor, such as Photoshop, try running a filter in incremental amounts over a still image. Try drawing the same artwork three times and it will appear to jitter subtly, or not so subtly depending on how much each version changes. Try changing the opacity over multiple images, and you'll create artwork that appears to "fade up." Try looking at existing animation on a VCR and single-framing it or try loading other people's animated GIFs into animating GIF programs to reverse-engineer what you like. Just be sure that reverse-engineering doesn't mean stealing. The same copyright laws that apply to images apply to movies!

note

Last Word Department

The web promises to be a place of change, with animation tools and options getting better and easier as the medium matures. Whichever animation tool and technology path you choose to travel, always keep your site's goals and audience in mind. Although animation can add a lot to your site's appeal, it can also create exclusionary walls that only the elite few with fast speed, loads of RAM, and high-end computers can break through. Make sure your medium fits your message; use animation wisely and sparingly, and the web will be a much more inviting place.

summary

Adding animation to a web site promises to offer more interest and appeal, but there are pitfalls, too. This chapter covered the aesthetics, technologies, and techniques of creating web-based animation content.

- Remember that anything that moves on your web page will draw the most attention to itself. Be sure that you animate content that you want to draw attention; otherwise you're detracting from information delivery that is more important.

- When you choose a technology for animation, keep in mind your audience and whether the medium fits the message. Realize that plug-ins require a lot of extra effort on the part of your audience and can sometimes exclude more visitors than invite.

- Animated GIFs are a great technology for offering animation of web pages. Make sure you study the information in this chapter that relates to looping, timing, and palette management. These issues bring forward some of the common pitfalls of animated GIF design.

8-Bit Graphics • A color or grayscale graphic or movie that has 256 colors or *less*.

16-Bit Graphics • A color image or movie that has 65,500 colors.

24-Bit Graphics • A color image or movie that has 16.7 million colors.

32-Bit Graphics • A color image or movie that has 16.7 million colors plus an 8-bit masking channel.

A

Adaptive Dithering • A form of dithering in which the program looks to the image to determine the best set of colors when creating an 8-bit or smaller palette. *See dithering.*

Aliasing • In bitmapped graphics, the jagged boundary along the edges of different-colored shapes within an image. *See anti-aliasing.*

Animated GIF • Part of the GIF89a spec that supports multiple images, and streams and displays them sequentially.

Anti-Aliasing • A technique for reducing the jagged appearance of aliased bitmapped images, usually by inserting pixels that blend at the boundaries between adjacent colors.

Artifacts • Image imperfections that are caused by compression.

Authoring Tools • Creation tools for interactive media.

AVI • Audio-Video Interleaved. Microsoft's file format for desktop video movies.

B

Bit Depth • The number of bits used to represent the color of each pixel in a given movie or still image. Specifically: bit depth of 2=black-and-white pixels; bit depth of 4=16 colors or grays; bit depth of 8=256 colors or grays; bit depth of 16=65,536 colors; bit depth of 24=(approximately) 16 million colors.

Bitmapped Graphics • Graphics that are pixel-based, as opposed to object-oriented. Bitmapped graphics are what the computer can display because it's a pixel-based medium, whereas object-oriented graphics can be viewed in high resolution once they are sent to a printer. Graphics on the web are bitmapped because they are viewed from a computer-screen-based delivery system.

Brightness • Adds white or tints an image, whereas lack of brightness adds black, or tones an image.

Browser • An application that enables you to access World Wide Web pages. Most browsers provide the capability to view web pages, copy and print material from web pages, download files from the web, and navigate throughout the web.

Browser-Safe Colors • These are the 216 colors that do not shift between platforms, operating systems, or most web browsers.

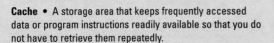

Cache • A storage area that keeps frequently accessed data or program instructions readily available so that you do not have to retrieve them repeatedly.

CGI • Common Gateway Interface. A web standard for extending the functionality of HTML. CGI always involves the combination of a live web server and external programming scripts.

Client • A computer that requests information from a network's server. *See server.*

Client Side • Client side means that the web element or effect can run locally off a computer and does not require the presence of a server.

Client-Side Imagemap • A client-side imagemap is programmed in HTML, and does not require a separate map definition file or to be stored on a live web server.

CLUT • Color LookUp Table. An 8-bit or lower image file uses a CLUT to define its palette.

Color Mapping • A color map refers to the color palette of an image. Color mapping means assigning colors to an image.

Color Names • Some browsers support using the name of a color instead of the color's hexadecimal value.

Compression • Reduction of the amount of data required to re-create an original file, graphic, or movie. Compression is used to reduce the transmission time of media and application files across the web.

Contrast • The degrees of separation between values.

D

Dithering • The positioning of different-colored pixels within an image that uses a 256-color palette to simulate a color that does not exist in the palette. A dithered image often looks noisy, or composed of scattered pixels. *See adaptive dithering.*

DPI • Dot Per Inch. A term used mostly by print graphics-based programs and professionals, and is a common measurement related to the resolution of an image. *See screen resolution.*

E

Extension • Abbreviated code at the end of a file that tells the browser what kind of file it's looking at. For example, a JPEG file would have the extension .jpg.

F

Fixed Palette • An established palette that is fixed. When a fixed palette web browser views images, it will convert images to its colors and not use the colors from the original.

FTP • File Transfer Protocol. The Internet protocol that enables users to remotely access files on other computers. FTP sites house files that can be downloaded to your computer system.

G

Gamma • Gamma measures the contrast that affects the midtones of an image. Adjusting the gamma lets you change the brightness values of the middle range of gray tones without dramatically altering the shadows and highlights.

Gamut • A viewable or printable color range.

GIF • A bitmapped color graphics file format. GIF is commonly used on the web because it employs an efficient compression method. *See JPEG.*

GIF89a • A type of GIF file that supports transparency and multi-blocks. Multi-blocks create the illusion of animation. GIF89a files are sometimes referred to as "transparent GIFs" or "animated GIFs."

H

Hexadecimal • A base-16 mathematics calculation, often used in scripts and code. Hexadecimal code is required by HTML to describe RGB values of color for the web.

HTML • HyperText Markup Language. The common language for interchange of hypertext between the World Wide Web client and server. Web pages must be written using HTML. *See hypertext.*

HTTP • HyperText Transfer Protocol is the protocol that the browser and the web server use to communicate with each other.

Hue • Defines a linear spectrum of the color wheel.

Hypertext • Text formatted with lines that enable the reader to jump among related topics. *See HTML.*

I

Imagemaps • Portions of images that are hypertext links. Using a mouse-based web client such as Netscape or Mosaic, the user clicks on different parts of a mapped image to activate different hypertext.

Inline Graphic • A graphic that sits inside an HTML document instead of the alternative, which requires that the image be downloaded and then viewed by using an outside system.

Interlaced GIFs • The GIF file format allows for "interlacing," which causes the GIF to load quickly at low or chunky resolution and then come into full or crisp resolution.

ISP • Acronym for Internet Service Provider.

J

JavaScript • A scripting language that enables you to extend the capabilities of HTML. Developed by Netscape.

JPEG • Acronym for Joint Photographic Experts Group, but commonly used to refer to a lossy compression technique that can reduce the size of a graphics file by as much as 96 percent. *See GIF.*

L

Links • Emphasized words in a hypertext document that act as pointers to more information on that specific subject. Links are generally underlined and may appear in a different color. When you click on a link, you can be transported to a different web site that contains information about the word or phrase used as the link. *See hypertext.*

Lossless Compression • A data compression technique that reduces the size of a file without sacrificing any of the original data. In lossless compression, the expanded or restored file is an exact replica of the original file before it was compressed. *See compression.*

Lossy Compression • A data compression technique in which some data is deliberately discarded to achieve massive reductions in the size of the compressed file.

M

Mask • The process of blocking out specific areas in a computer graphic.

MIME • Multipurpose Internet Mail Extensions. An Internet standard for transferring nontext-based data such as sounds, movies, and images.

Moiré • A pattern that results when dots overlap. This problem often occurs when scanning printed materials.

O

Object-Oriented Graphics • A graphic image composed of objects such as lines, circles, ellipses, and boxes that can be moved independently. This type of graphic is used for print-based design because it can be printed at a higher resolution than a computer screen. *See bitmapped graphics.*

P

Passive Navigation • Animation, slide shows, streaming movies, and audio. Basically anything that plays without the end user initiating the content.

Plug-In • Plug-ins are supported by some browsers, and extend the capability of standard HTML. They need to be installed in the end user's plug-in folder, found inside the browser software folder.

PNG • An acronym for Portable Network Graphics. PNG is a lossless file format that supports interlacing, 8-bit transparency, and gamma information.

PostScript • A sophisticated page description language used for printing high-quality text and graphics on laser printers and high-resolution printing devices.

Primary Colors • The theory behind primary colors is that these colors are the starting point from which any other colors can be mixed. On the computer, the primary colors are red, green, and blue because color mixing is additive (created with light). With pigment, the primary colors are red, blue, and yellow because color mixing is subtractive.

Progressive JPEG • A type of JPEG that produces an interlaced effect as it loads and can be 30% smaller than standard JPEGs. Not currently supported by many web browsers.

Q-R

QuickTime • System software developed by Apple Computer for presentation of desktop video.

Rollover • A type of navigation button that changes when the end user's mouse rolls over it.

S

Saturation • Defines the intensity of color.

Screen Resolution • Screen resolution generally refers to the resolution of common computer monitors. 72 dpi is an agreed upon average, although you will also hear of 96 dpi being the resolution of larger displays.

Search Engine • A type of application, commonly found on the web, that enables you to search by keywords for information or URLs.

Server • A computer that provides services for users of its network. The server receives requests for services and manages the requests so that they are answered in an orderly manner. *See client.*

Server Push • Server push is the method of requesting images or data from the server and automating their playback. It involves CGI and the presence of a live web server.

Server Side • Server side means any type of web page element that depends on being loaded to a server. It also implies the use of a CGI script.

Server-Side Imagemap • A server-side imagemap requires that the information about the imagemap be saved within a "map definition file" that needs to be stored on a server and accessed by a CGI script.

Splash Screen • The main menu screen or opening graphic to a web page.

Sprite • An individual component of an animation, such as a character or graphic that moves independently.

T-U

Tables • Tables create rows and columns, as in a spreadsheet, and can be used to align data and images.

Tags • ASCII text indicators with which you surround text and images to designate certain formats or styles.

Transparent GIFs • A subset of the original GIF file format that adds header information to the GIF file, which notes that a defined color will be masked out.

True Color • The quality of color provided by 24-bit color depth. 24-bit color depth results in 16.7 million colors, which is usually more than adequate for the human eye.

URL • Uniform Resource Locator. A web site address.

V-W

Value • The range from light to dark in an image.

WYSIWYG • Pronounced wizzy-wig. A design philosophy in which formatting commands directly affects the text displayed on-screen so that the screen shows the appearance of printed text.

Symbols

229

B

H

J-K

234

237

<deconstructing web graphics>
Web Design Case Studies and Tutorials

Deconstructing Web Graphics profiles top web designers and programmers in order to demystify and analyze how they make decisions, solve complex issues, and create exceptional web sites. Adding her own voice and digital design teaching experience to the book, best-selling author Lynda Weinman selects from her list of favorite designed web sites. She walks you through how to read and understand the source code for each page, breaks down all of the technical elements, and describes the inside details straight from the designers and programmers who created the pages.

This conversational and information-rich guide offers insight into web design that is not found through any other means. Profiles of successful web designers, programmers, photographers, and illustrators allow them to share their tips, techniques, and recommendations. You'll bring your own web design skills to a higher level through studying their experiences and the step-by-step tutorials and examples found in *Deconstructing Web Graphics*.

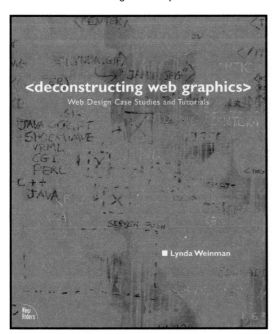

In this book, you'll learn about:

- Low-bandwidth graphics
- Scanned imagery for the web
- Cross-platform colors
- Custom Photoshop brushes and patterns
- Artwork using ASCII
- Copyright issues
- Animated GIFs
- LOWSRC animation tricks
- Tables for alignment
- Invisible GIFs for spacers
- Frames for navigation
- HTML tricks and workarounds
- Java
- JavaScript
- CGI
- Forms processing
- Server push
- Client pull
- Shockwave and Macromedia Director
- Sound and video files
- VRML

Product and Sales Information

Deconstructing Web Graphics
By Lynda Weinman
ISBN: 1-56205-641-7 ▪ $44.99/USA ▪ 250 pages
Available at your local bookstore or online
Macmillan Publishing ▪ 1-800-428-5331
- http://www.mcp.com/newriders
- http://www.lynda.com

\<coloring web graphics\>

Master Color and Image File Formats for the Web

Written by Lynda Weinman and Bruce Heavin, this book features practical advice that will help you greatly expand your color web graphic design skills. The purpose of this book is to help artists, programmers, and hobbyists understand how to work with color and image file formats for web delivery. Web browsers and different operating systems handle color in specific ways that many web designers aren't aware of.

A color palette of 216 browser-safe colors is identified and organized to help web designers confidently select successful cross-platform color choices and combinations. The book includes sections on color theory and understanding web color file formats as well as step-by-step tutorials that explain how to work with browser-safe colors in Photoshop, Paint Shop Pro, Photo-Paint, Painter, FreeHand, and Illustrator. The cross-platform CD-ROM includes hundreds of suggested color combinations for web page design, as well as hundreds of palettes and browser-safe clip art files.

In this book, you'll learn to:

- Create colors in your artwork that won't shift or dither across multiple platforms
- Choose web-appropriate color schemes for your page designs
- Create many browser-safe hybrid variations
- Use Photoshop, Paint Shop Pro, Photo-Paint, FreeHand, Illustrator, and Director to manage web-specific color

The cross-platform CD-ROM includes:

- Browser-safe color palettes
- Browser-safe color swatches for Photoshop and other imaging programs
- Browser-safe colors organized by hue, value, and saturation
- Browser-safe color clip art for web use
- Electronic versions of color swatches grouped as they are in the book
- Sample HTML pages with recommended color groupings
- Sample patterns, backgrounds, buttons, and rules

Product and Sales Information

Coloring Web Graphics
By Lynda Weinman and Bruce Heavin
ISBN: 1-56205-669-7 ▪ $50.00/USA ▪ 258 pages
(+CD-ROM) Available at your local bookstore or
online ▪ Macmillan Publishing ▪ 1-800-428-5331
- http://www.mcp.com/newriders
- http://www.lynda.com